snap, crackle or stop

THE ONLY
DO IT – IS

WAY TO
TO DO IT

snap, crackle or stop

change your career and create your own destiny

Barbara E. Quinn

www.yourmomentum.com
the stuff that drives you

What is momentum?

Momentum is a completely new publishing philosophy, in print and online, dedicated to giving you more of the information, inspiration and drive to enhance who you are, what you do, and how you do it.

Fusing the changing forces of work, life and technology, momentum will give you the bright stuff for a brighter future and set you on the way to being all you can be.

Who needs momentum?

Momentum is for people who want to make things happen in their career and their life, who want to work at something they enjoy and that's worthy of their talent and their time.

Momentum people have values and principles, and question who they are, what they do, and who for. Wherever they work, they want to feel proud of what they do. And they are hungry for information, stimulation, ideas and answers ...

Momentum online

Visit *www.yourmomentum.com* to be part of the talent community. Here you'll find a full listing of current and future books, an archive of articles by momentum authors, sample chapters and self-assessment tools. While you're there, post your worklife questions to our momentum coaches and sign up to receive free newsletters with even more stuff to drive you.

More momentum

If you need more drive for your life, try one of these titles, all published under the momentum label:

change activist
make big things happen fast
Carmel McConnell

lead yourself
be where others will follow
Mick Cope

happy mondays
put the pleasure back into work
Richard Reeves

the big difference
life works when you choose it
Nicola Phillips

hey you!
pitch to win in an ideas world
Will Murray

innervation
wire yourself for the new economy
Guy Browning

float you
how to capitalize on your talent
Carmel McConnell & Mick Cope

coach yourself
make real change in your life
Anthony M. Grant & Jane Greene

from here to e
equip yourself for a career in the wired economy
Lisa Khoo

grow your human capital
what you know, who you know, how you use it
Hilarie Owen

PEARSON EDUCATION LIMITED

Head Office
Edinburgh Gate
Harlow CM20 2JE
Tel: +44 (0)1279 623623
Fax: +44 (0)1279 431059

London Office:
128 Long Acre, London WC2E 9AN
Tel: +44 (0)20 7447 2000
Fax: +44 (0)20 7240 5771
Website: www.business-minds.com

First published in Great Britain in 2001

ISBN 1843 04007 7

British Library Cataloguing in Publication Data
A CIP catalogue record for this book can be obtained from the British Library.

10 9 8 7 6 5 4 3 2 1

Typeset by Northern Phototypesetting Co. Ltd, Bolton
Printed and bound in Great Britain by Biddles Ltd, Guildford and King's Lynn

Cover design by Heat
Concept text design by Heat
Production text design by Claire Brodmann
Book Designs, Lichfield, Staffs

The Publishers' policy is to use paper manufactured from sustainable forests.

snap, crackle or stop

momentum

to my husband Marc Besner for fuelling my dream.

about the author…

Barbara Quinn started her career as a clerk in a university. She worked her way up the corporate ladder by moving between jobs and companies while completing her Bachelor of Arts and Master's Degree in the evening. Her last corporate job was as director and vice-president of human resources for Levi Strauss and Company – the best job ever. Sensing something undone in her career, she gave up the job to travel in Europe and the Caribbean for a year. Nine months later, as the money ran out, she went back home and created a sign saying 'consultant for hire.'

Barbara then went on to be a founding partner of CAIL Consulting Group Inc., a very successful management consulting firm. Her biggest accomplishment so far is co-authoring the book *Shared Services: Mining for Corporate Gold* that has been on the business bestseller list in Canada for a year and was voted the overall No. 2 book for the year 2000.

To celebrate, she bought an old 380SL Mercedes Benz sports car. Her licence plates read: DES10E (Destiny), in honour of this book and the ideals of finding your passion. barb@barbquinn.com

thank you…

to June Dagnall for her enthusiasm and research of some great interview candidates.

to Anne Reece for her passion and in-depth research on the topic of destiny and career change.

to Lee Wood, *coachmarla@lifepathcreations.com*, Kaile Warren, Rhonda Lashen, Peter Beyak, Maarten and Nadina Schaddellee, Martin and Lee-Ann Pentony-Woolwich, Richard Craze, Su Grimmer, Ken Read, Mark Rowswell (Dashan to his Chinese fans), Leo Klus, James Kirsch, Bonnie Stern, Christopher and Charleen Noto, Michael Ross, Bruce and Nancy Pon, James Kirsch, Steven Chasens.

chapter one
changing careers and mastering your own destiny

chapter two
snap, crackle or stop:
a state of mind

chapter three
snap

---

chapter four
crackle

opening

snap, crackle or stop

momentum

chapter five
stop

---

more on letting go / 66

chapter six
where are you in your career?

don't run away from what you want, run to it / 84

opening

snap, crackle or stop

momentum

chapter seven
where would you rather be?

chapter eight
the intangible dynamics to mastering destiny

opening

snap, crackle or stop

momentum

chapter nine
power tools for action

chapter ten
snap, crackle or stop: the finale

01

chapter one
changing careers and mastering your own destiny

be inspired to master your own destiny

I am convinced we have the power to master our own destiny. It all comes down to choosing passion over the ordinary and for accepting that our fate is what we make it. Mastering destiny is a time in our career when we are working for expression, when a job is not a job but a deep opportunity to express ourselves. Do you think you are mastering your own destiny? Do you believe that you are where you are supposed to be?

Imagine being invited to a game of career poker. Each of us is dealt a hand of cards: skills, experience, education and desire. A deck of opportunities lies in the middle of the table. If you think destiny is preordained, then wait and see what the next card brings. When you are sitting in exactly the same place, same job, same time next year, you can sit back and take comfort in fate.

If, on the other hand, you want to develop the attitude and skills to master your own destiny, then get into the game and take charge. People who are working in their field of passion feel lucky, imagining they stumbled on it. Scratch a little deeper and you will find that they really made it happen. They took at least one step that got them closer.

You may be dreaming of quitting your job and running away to a cabin in the woods. Think again. That is called retirement. I am talking about making deliberate decisions, changing careers and finding work that makes you happy. It is not for ever since destiny is not one destination. You will have to make these changes many times in your life. When people hear the word destiny, they think of preordained fate and talent: the brilliant young mathematics student, the superior athlete or child genius at piano. These rare examples feed the myth that destiny is preordained, as though there is some gigantic career map with your name attached to a job out there in the universe – Lee Smith, accountant for life: Mary Wooster, engineer for infinity; Jon Singh, technical analyst for ever. Not so; it all comes down to choice.

We owe it to ourselves to discover and use our talents.

The goal is to find opportunities for work related to what we love to do, what we've always dreamed of doing. It means continually evolving and switching work patterns to find as many outlets for our talent as we can fit in during a lifetime. Like a great painter, there is no one piece of art that sums up a lifetime. An artist's work and style may change considerably over the years, the artistic techniques and processes may be different but the need for expression remains constant. Imagine if the great impressionist painter, Paul Cézanne, had not quit law practice to paint. Hard to imagine the world being robbed of his great talent and legacy. He might have been a great lawyer but he was a greater painter. Ultimately the desire to master one's own destiny is rooted in the need to find happiness in and through work. It comes from a sense of knowing that there is something important to be done and that you are the one who is supposed to be doing it. Do you feel you are hitting your stride? How do you feel when someone asks what you do for a living? Tinker, tailor, soldier, sailor! Is this what you want? If you do nothing to make the change, nothing is what you'll get. Significantly, the change process starts with unhappiness and restlessness, a deep longing for another kind of career.

You are not alone if you are feeling dissatisfied with a job that does not make best use of your talents. In an exclusive survey of Britain's managers, one in three is dissatisfied, one in five is downright unhappy. A US Gallup poll, conducted in 1999, revealed that only 39 per cent of working adults are completely satisfied with their jobs. Another North American survey claims that 85 per cent of the workforce are disillusioned with their jobs and nearly 50 per cent suffer from physical or emotional burnout. So what is wrong? Are the jobs really all that bad? Is it that people have not found their groove? I think so. I believe people who feel burned out from their careers are bored. They might be busy but they are essentially bored. Their job feels like a prison sentence. Doing time!

My husband told me on our honeymoon that I could do and be anything I wanted to. No one had ever said this to me before. This was foreign language to me then and it is to many people now. We have a hard time accepting the fact that we can do anything. The only thing stopping us is us. There are some people who have given up on the idea that change is worth the effort. You've met them at work. They're so unhappy in their jobs, their negativity spills out into the room. I remember a man who worked in a utility. He had a white board in his cubicle. Walking by one day, I asked what the number was in the right-hand corner of his white board – 4015. Without a blink, he said it was the number of days until retirement and that every morning his ritual with coffee was to subtract one day. He was serious when he said this is what gave him a glimmer of hope to get through the day. As he departs this life, will he wonder if he could or should have done something else?

This is not a tale of how to be a millionaire nor is it a fable on the benefits of a sparse but spiritual lifestyle. Not that money should be seen as trifling. Getting paid for doing what we love almost seems like a bonus at times.

Mastering destiny is not about becoming rich or poor.

Mastering destiny may mean more money than you ever dreamed of. The fact is when you love what you do, you are somehow very good at it. When you're good at something, you get rewarded. Think of working in an area where you pour your whole energy, intellect and heart into it. Don't you think this will give you returns? Enthusiasm is noticed. Clients see it. Bosses see it. People that count notice when someone is passionate about what they do. It's too hard to fake.

Many people have been successful beyond their wildest dreams. They didn't set out to be rich. Although it looks like luck, it was really choice. And yes, it involved risk. They were open to opportunity and, for the most part, walked through the door and put their heads down. There is no such thing as easy money.

For others, mastering destiny may mean finding work that pays less but offers bigger returns in happiness and satisfaction. There are many people who make a clear choice of happiness over money. They scale back and down. They decide to need less money and more fun. We all need money but sometimes it just isn't enough. Going through the motions in a dull job is tiring and no amount of consumerism makes up for it. Oh sure, it's fun to go and spend money to compensate for work that has zero satisfaction, but we all know that short-lived feeling. Many people feel tied down and chained to their career because of the money. Over time, this is a recipe for disaster. Either you will burn out because your heart's not in it or you'll find yourself in the wrong place on the career ladder, feeling like you are never really getting ahead. And it's because you're not. If I am making good money but am terribly unhappy, how rich am I? I am not advocating quitting work, having nothing to eat and sitting around waiting for a divine light to show itself. I am saying that it comes down to choice. Living for passion or not.

Carly Fiorina, chairman and CEO of Hewlett-Packard, has been on the power 50 list of top women for three years running. She got there because of her passion, not because she mechanically plotted her rise to the top. Her goal isn't just leadership, it's transformation through inspiration.

Mastering destiny is a responsibility and a choice

I believe we have a fundamental responsibility as humans to discover the career that matches up perfectly with what we want to do and what we are good at doing. It feels irresponsible to choose anything other than a career of self-expression yet many of us accept less than what we want and deserve because we are choosing not to find our destiny. The pursuit of a fantastic career is not only desirable, it is essential. No matter what age, what location, what family or job history, anyone can get to the state of mastering destiny if it is taken on as a responsibility not a possibility.

George Lucas, master filmmaker and creator of the *Star Wars* series, describes the power of taking responsibility in your own hands. In his first year of film school, he explained that students often sat around the cafeteria wondering out loud, even whining, about when they would be given a chance to make a real movie. In the meantime, each student was provided with one minute's worth of film to test out the huge and cumbersome animation camera, as a way of learning the mechanics of the camera. George, unlike the rest of his class, chose to turn that little piece of film into a one-minute movie. Subsequently, this tiny movie won all kinds of awards at film festivals for the innovation of using an animation camera to shoot live action. He had learned the power of responsibility over possibility.

James Cameron, the award-winning director of the blockbuster film *Titanic*, made the same point when he advised 'wannabe' filmmakers to just pick up a camera and start shooting:

'Don't wait to be asked because nobody is going to ask you and don't wait for the perfect conditions, they'll never be perfect. You have to take the plunge and start shooting even if it's bad. You can always hide it but you will have learned something.'

James Cameron

There are many people stuck in a career or company that has somehow become less than enchanting. Either they feel undervalued, underwhelmed by the lack of challenge or hopeless about the possibility of change. We don't want mediocrity and a pay cheque, we want our contribution to make a real impact. On the other hand, some people are overwhelmed by too many demands. A recent survey indicated that approximately half of the workforce is experiencing burnout. The question is as a result of what? I suspect boredom. Or working at something that just doesn't give back – energy in and not a lot of emotional return out.

Most of us have a need to be part of something great and fulfilling.

When in my own depths of corporate depression, I had a fantasy that kept me going when times were tough and that was to own a bookstore. I used to dream of how easy my life would be standing at the cash register, surrounded by beloved books. Instead of corporate meetings and politics, I used to imagine this wonderful life of simplicity. 'Would you like a bag? That will be $16.98 please.' No complex interactions. Being an unabashed book lover who can spend hours in a bookstore, I pictured the fun of unpacking boxes filled with shiny new book jackets. I actually confided this fantasy to one of my corporate peers during an offsite meeting where we secretly discussed what we would be doing if we weren't being executives. He then proceeded to tell me what a hassle it was owning a bookstore, that his wife owned one, at which point I interrupted him and said, 'Look Harry, please shut up. It's my fantasy and you're messing with it.' Dreams can keep us going for a long time but eventually they become more tiring than inspirational. The lack of action wears us down. About one year later, he had been fired and I quit my corporate executive job to take an eight-month trip in the Caribbean and Europe with a plan to start a consulting practice upon my return. Owning a bookstore wasn't my actual destiny but it was a great escape. I didn't yet know my real destiny was to actually write one of those books with the shiny jackets.

Mastering destiny doesn't involve a crystal ball nor is it a one-step, two-step mechanical system. Any person, whatever their size, shape or age, can take control in this way. It is not about being perfect, being the best, the smartest or the most talented. How many times have you looked at successful people and thought to yourself that they weren't the most talented, wondering how they got to where they got to. Why did they? Because they took charge and crafted their careers one step at a time.

You're stuck where you enter.

If you are ambitious, you will have to move to get attention since you are often constrained by the level at which you enter a company. People at the top of their careers believe you have to change companies if you want to really get ahead. The days of 'one company' experience are long gone.

Although there are guides, coaches, muses and gurus, in the end you and you alone will have to choose mastering destiny as a career state. You can make a living doing what you really want to. It is possible. You can break free of the invisible chains holding you down in a job and a place that does not use your talents, wit, skills and ambition. Although it may be fun to fantasize about slinging hamburgers for a change, it would be an ultimate tragedy for you if you don't manage to find a way to live your destiny and make money at the same time. Maybe you feel stifled in your current career, not getting ahead fast enough. So what are you going to do about it?

The harder you work, the luckier you are

A successful screenwriter being interviewed was asked for his secret to success. The screenwriter nodded and replied, 'I find if I actually sit down and write a screenplay, I stand a better chance of selling it.' To wit, he had hit on one of the ways to achieve change and that is simply to do it. Many of us think about doing something differently but often don't act. The screenwriter didn't go around saying I want to be a screenwriter, he wrote the plays. Luck had nothing to do with it.

Finding destiny involves hard work and determination.

No discussion on destiny can be complete without examining the idea of luck. Most people who are fulfilled in their work, do believe they are lucky. But what does luck mean? It doesn't mean sitting around waiting for a knock at the door, a phone call or an e-mail with an offer to find destiny. Although many of us feel very lucky doing the right kind of work, the kind that is fun and fulfilling, outsiders would frequently describe us as hard working. Perhaps the old adage is true that the harder you work, the luckier you are. Not very sexy but there it is. Work that is in tune with our destiny is still work. The difference, when doing work in the destiny line, is that it is fun.

Bonnie Stern, one of Canada's leading chefs, with several award-winning cookbooks and a national television show, has spent some thirty years working her craft. She did not sit around dreaming about being famous, she just devoted herself to working the craft and having fun doing it. Bonnie reminds us that cooking is hard work and asks us to consider that out of the approximately 4,000 chefs in any major city, only 20 of them have any kind of name recognition or fame. The other 3,880 chefs are working hard each night, putting great food out, doing their best and working at the business for passion and expression. By the way, Bonnie was headed to be a professional librarian until she had the courage to quit university and follow her passion for cooking, never realizing that it would lead to such phenomenal success.

Very few people will admit to being lazy. As a matter of fact, everyone seems to go around bragging about just how busy they are. The question is busy at what? If you don't take time to work at your craft and your dream, then it is unlikely you will be anywhere different next year. I like to think of it as working hard on your future. Destiny work on the whole is not a nine-to-five affair; it's more like a consuming passion than an afterthought.

There is no time like the present

There has never been a better time for taking charge and controlling your own career. The current shortage of talent means a shift in power from employer to employee. Although there is an abundance of capital funds, there is a shortage of intellectual capital. If you are a knowledge worker, you've got what companies want. Companies are fighting for scarce talent. Individuals are even hiring their own agents as if part of the Hollywood star system.

What are you waiting for?

The battle for talent means companies will have to learn flexibility and humility if they want to attract and keep you. This will mean creative people policies that enable you to pursue your destiny while working, it will mean a return to taking company-sponsored courses and education that is in line with your interests not your job. It could mean arranged sabbaticals or leaves of absence to pursue interests or deep passions, such as working to help developing countries, installing water systems in war-torn parts of the world, taking film classes, studying art or cooking in France. Companies are going to have to open up their minds about work because of the shortage of talent so there is no better time than the present to consider how you can find your destiny. Quitting a job and taking time out is not only possible, it's less risky than it has ever been, especially for people in the knowledge business. There will be other jobs out there if you need one.

There is a quiet revolution simmering in many corporate jobs, consulting careers and professions among people who are starting to poke their heads up and look for something more meaningful than just a way to make money. There is an increasing demand for work that offers learning and insight. More and more people are beginning to actively search for meaning, questioning whether they have found their passion. Corporate executives and consultants are going to new start-up companies and gambling with the new economy. Many women are choosing entrepreneurship, starting up companies and creating their own future. Something is happening and it is the beginning of the curve.

Look at the media. *Fast Company* magazine, national business newspapers, television shows are all covering stories about people who have left traditional jobs for the excitement of something new. It has become a 'hot' topic – to examine and explore success stories, people who are living their vision. When was the last time you saw an interview featuring the story of an employee who has been with his company for 25 years? There are lots of people in this category incidentally but the media buzz isn't interested, neither are the readers or watchers. We want drama. We want dreams.

Eat the damn chocolate bar

You might be wondering how an engineer from a little town of 500 in Saskatchewan got involved selling expensive box seats and sponsorships for world 'open tennis' events in Shanghai, China. A dream job involving travel, excitement and challenge, especially for someone who loves sports! You might be wondering unless you knew Nancy Pon, who at 29 has already figured out how to keep moving until you find that 'missing thing'. At 10 years old, Nancy remembers telling people that she planned on being an artist and they'd reply, 'Ya, ya, but what are you really going to be?' So guess what, she stuffed that idea and studied engineering only to discover that she in fact hated it. She did graduate though, by the skin of her teeth, and took a nice engineering job in a transportation company. A few years later the money idea wore off, and restlessness set in. So she up and packed her bags to go to professional art school a few thousand miles from home. Eight months later, and a little bit disillusioned with the world of academic art, she went back to her old transportation job.

Engineering by day and art on the weekends, friends helped her mount her own art exhibition where she sold a whopping 32 out of 35 paintings. She still felt something was missing. Snap, she up and quit to study mandarin at a language school in Beijing. This led her to land a high profile job with the American Chamber of Commerce in Shanghai where she just left for her current position. To outsiders,

Nancy makes this change look easy, but inside she knows the agony and frustration needed to step out of the comfort zone and make bold moves. As she says, it's like having a craving for a chocolate bar. You might first talk yourself out of the calories by eating a cracker. Not quite satisfied, you might try a juicy plum. Still not satisfied, you might have some carrot sticks. You are all filled up, there is no space left, but you know what – you still want the damn chocolate bar.

Nancy is learning to trust her instincts and follow her passion. If the job doesn't provide expression, she has learned to move on. She's not fearless, she's just learned to have faith in her own talent and skills.

Sidebar to the story

Nancy has learned how to take control of her own career. She has done this by letting her feelings out on the table and admitting when she isn't happy or satisfied. Nancy keeps her eye on the long term and is prepared to make short-term sacrifices to get what she wants. No whining, she puts her head down and makes a plan. She credits her success to people helping her. Really, I believe it's because she is admired for her ability to run towards what she wants.

I don't know what to be

Don't let the question 'but what work, what job?' get in the way. Although if you do you're in good company, since many people feel this is the biggest stumbling block to making change. Granted, it is part of the challenge. The key to figuring out the 'what' lies in your energy and motivation to carry out a self-assessment. What skills do you have and what do you love doing? Sometimes they're not the same. I might be good at something but hate doing it and vice versa.

Getting to the 'what' might also require a suspension of logic for the moment. The rational world says you have to know what before you decide to change. The intuitive world says, first decide to change,

snap, crackle or stop

momentum

and then see what happens. Have faith, trust the process. If you do the work, you'll come to some conclusions about what you really want to do or what you've always dreamed of doing. A lot of career decisions come about from sheer openness to change. When we are open to possibilities and ready for change, they often pop up. I think we project our desires.

The hard work has to start with you. No one else can tell you. Deep down you probably know or could describe your fantasy job. Sooner or later, you are going to have to admit it out loud to someone.

Step right up and examine your career. How does it measure up? Are you happy? Does your job provide you with the right outlet for expression? Have you found the place that is exciting, that uses your talents? Are you 100 per cent committed to your life? Have you hit your stride?

What I hope this book will do

I want you to be inspired by people who are mastering their own destiny. This is not a self-help book, it is a book of inspiration – one that will help you get up, step out and make that change you've been thinking about. I hope you will be energized enough to take that first step towards your own future. I want you to become motivated enough to go and explore, to have an excellent career adventure.

Later on in this book you will have an opportunity to complete an inventory (see Appendix 1) that shows where you are in your career. It will give you some ways to confirm what you are feeling and provide you with a platform for change. You'll have a good sense of what you need to do to get going.

I hope you can accept the idea that your career can be as unique as your thumbprint. You can invent a career that uses your skills, talent and aspirations. You don't have to radically transform your life. You just have to think about what you want and take that one step every day every week that gets you closer. If every day, all you do is look at a post-it note that has your vision written on it. Good. That's something.

Read the patterns. You are in charge of your own career. If you don't take charge, who will? If you haven't found your passion, you're not looking hard enough or in the right places. If you are thwarted in your expression, and can't find the right outlet, what are you going to do about it? How are you going to make sure you are not in the same place, next year? How are you going to make sure you are exactly where you want to be?

Stop worrying about what and where. Here's what you have to do:

◆ Say out loud, I'm going to change, I will.

◆ Take one step tomorrow and make your future a habit.

◆ Be open to possibilities – let go and see what happens.

◆ Stay motivated.

◆ Don't give in to complacency. Being average is tragic.

If you want to find a career that is more in line with your aspirations, come along and find the momentum to change. You can be what you want if you choose to. It all depends on your state of mind: snap, crackle or stop.

chapter two
snap, crackle or stop:
a state of mind

what is your state of mind – snap, crackle or stop?

It is unlikely that on the last day of work, we will ask ourselves if we should have worked harder. It isn't the working, it is what we've been working at, that will make all the difference.

Are you fed up, ready to snap? Have you come to that point in your life when you know it's time to move on? Do you find yourself getting cynical and settling for good is good enough? Or, have you let go? Are you going through the motions at work, knowing that you and work are not connected in the least? Let's see what state you are in.

Snap – it's over

Coming to that moment in your life when you know that it's time to move on is an emotional reaction. Logic, facts and figures do not add up to a tidy formula. There is no simple exercise or checklist that will determine if you are unhappy enough or fed up enough to snap. Dissatisfaction often takes a long time to take hold. For some, it may be like a slow drip of water into a gigantic oak barrel. Simple requests on the job become major tasks. Routine business trips are seen as about as much fun as getting a voluntary root canal. At meetings, you may find your eyeballs glazing over. You lose track of the agenda and don't even care. You start making lists, shopping lists, things to do, names and notes. To survive, you have to start acting. A friend of mine who left a lucrative career in consulting at the age of 45, described her last few months as 'trying hard to stay awake in the face of complete and utter irrelevancy.'

For others, it comes at lightning speed, quite unconsciously or even as a complete surprise. Blow-ups and hastily written resignation letters come out of the blue. Frustration may come gushing out as if from nowhere. The man in the story I am about to tell you is real. He is the inspiration for this book. I have no idea where he is today.

Snap: Waking up in Papua New Guinea

The story begins in Athens. My husband and I took a day trip to visit the famous oracle at Delphi, the place where ancient Greeks fell down in front of the oracle to ask her divine questions about the future. This most unlikely place gave me a story from a man whom I met casually. Then again, it is always strangers who open up and tell life stories to other strangers, knowing perhaps the inevitable truth that you will never meet the person again. So it was over a lovely lunch in the hot Greek sun, one day in May 1986 that I learned something important about destiny. The man sat calmly beside his wife as we fiddled with our menus and contemplated roast lamb or perhaps a nice kebab. I asked him the inevitable question about what he did for a living. He started with an exciting story of having just spent ten years as a manager of a coffee plantation in Papua New Guinea. Obviously British from the accent, I jokingly asked what a Brit was doing in New Guinea? This was glossed over initially as my husband and I were regaled with tales of unimaginable adventure and terror. His wife and he lived high in the mountains in a provided-for plantation house. For ten years they slept with rifles under their bed and that was only the beginning. Tales of bribery and corruption, fights and eruptions of violence by the coffee pickers were only tidbits of the whole story. It sounded awful but exciting.

The part I was still curious about in this whole story, apart from the obvious adventure, was how they had ended up there. When he realized we were genuinely interested in the journey, he then told us about his life in England. He and his wife had a very comfortable existence. He had an excellent job as a commercial real estate agent in a very large and prosperous firm. He was more than an up-and-comer, he was at the top of his career and had made many prosperous deals for the firm. Then he stumbled on the deal of a lifetime. It was a prospect that involved several millions of pounds. He was driven, he was excited, he was single-minded. The firm encouraged him, offering him resources, support and anything else he would need to make this deal succeed. He worked the client, he entertained, he relentlessly built relationships and connections. This consumed his life for three long years. Three years is a long time to focus on one deal. And then, like a gift from the gods, it landed.

That day he phoned his wife screaming with joy. He was a hero at the company. He told his wife he would be back very late since the president and top executives were taking him out for a night he would never forget. And he never did forget it. Champagne, more champagne, drinks, a sumptuous meal, vintage wines and copious amounts of port accompanied laughter and the delicious feeling of being with people who at that particular moment are totally ecstatic with you. This partying went on into the wee hours of the night. His wife was thrilled for him. When he got home, she heard him come in even though she herself was in a deep sleep. As she rose to consciousness, she heard a sound she could not identify. Listening carefully as she tried to rise out of a deep sleep, she suddenly opened her eyes and ears to her husband bent over the bed sobbing deeply and convulsed in obvious grief and sadness. She could not reconcile this image with the earlier phone call and with a sinking heart thought that the magic deal had evaporated. But no, it had not. That was the point her husband kept saying to her in between sobs. He just kept saying how useless it all was, how he had spent so much of his life devoted to this single deal and that there was really no point to it all. He could go on no longer. He felt like something had snapped. He had to get out, he could never do this again to himself.

His wife, like the president and the executive of the company, dismissed this thinking over the next few days as a simple depression, something he would surely get over. And true enough, most people do experience this kind of dip, this kind of valley of depression after a major euphoria or success beyond imagination. Most people do not act on it, they instead wait it out. Not this guy! No, two weeks later, he just up and quit. Gasps all the way around and this man with a young family. Snap, he spied a job in a London newspaper for a plantation manager in Papua New Guinea. He applied and got it. One month later he and his wife, and children, were packing up to move to a place they had never been to before, to a job he knew nothing about, to a culture and environment that the word foreign simply does not adequately describe.

He has never looked back. At the end of our meal, they told us they were now on the way to Australia to see what they would see and they sure looked happy. He was fortunate to have a partner who had been willing to go along and live in such a remote and even potentially dangerous location. Having made this dramatic move, they felt that moving to Australia was a virtual piece of cake even though they had no connections, no family and no immediate prospects.

Sidebar to the story

This man had the guts to accept his state of mind and change careers. It would have been all too easy to justify sticking around but his courage to just snap and act helped him develop the skills to master his own destiny. He developed resilience for sure. He knew he was empowered to make his own decisions and did not have to rely on anyone for direction or inspiration. He had no fears about walking into the unknown and finding work that would not only intrigue him but also allow him to make a great living. He is probably still in Australia having a wonderful life.

Have you snapped yet?

The following questions, when answered honestly, should indicate to you whether or not you have snapped yet:

- Are you bored most of the time at work?
- What career ideas have recently popped into your head?
- Are you feeling more depressed than normal by your job?
- Do you feel 'fried' by your job?
- Do you find yourself being angry a lot of the time?
- Do you find yourself envying others who leave?

Sometimes a snap isn't even negative. It can be an idea that pops into your head. The difference is most of us think without actually acting.

Take Perween Warsi, founder of S&A Foods in England. She trusted her own feeling that there were no decent samosas in the supermarkets. She had faith and trusted in her own ability to make a better samosa and acted on it. Today her business is worth $35 million. The details are only important if you are looking for an excuse not to snap into action.

Crackle – an underlying rumble of discontent

Most of us are probably here: career greyness. Some days are good and some not so good. Good ones keep us rooted in the same place, grateful even for the opportunity. Other days we might find unbearable for the boredom or nagging dissatisfaction. Over time, the more cracks, the more we feel compelled to move. The middle of the see-saw becomes an impossible place to stay for any length of time: snap or stop, something has to give.

We are all pretty good at justifying the status quo. Just when you seem at the end of your rope and ready for a move, some tiny little morsel of hope is presented. A new project, a new boss, a fat raise or stock options dangling in front of your nose, all offering up the possibility of staying put and making do. Sometimes money provides temporary sanity.

When the energy and fun goes, there go I.

In the long run though, it's passion that keeps us consumed. When the energy and fun goes, no amount of money is a substitute. We might find pleasant diversions such as great vacations, new cars and lots of toys, but in the long run, if the work isn't satisfying, the nagging feeling comes back to haunt us. What is the point of hanging in when the job does not offer enough of what we're looking for? At the beginning of our working life, most of us are pretty happy to just get money. Later, we begin to want more. We also start to meld our identity with what we do for a living. You know the drill. You're at a party and the first thing out of the stranger's mouth is the coy question 'and what do you do for a living?'

When we are young, grown-ups mean well but are somehow annoying when they ask 'And what do you want to be when you grow up?' So we learn to play the game for a long time, answering primly with what little we know at the time – fireman, nurse, fighter pilot, teacher. Nice and simple. Little people don't say management consultant, middle manager, systems analyst, acquisitions editor. Jobs that exist today didn't even have a name two or three years ago. The point is most of us drift into our careers. We experiment, get summer jobs, meet people, go to school and somehow end up creating a career in a particular line of work. The beginning of our career is easy because most of us don't expect too much except to get money for our effort. Newspaper deliveries, chambermaid and construction jobs, waiter, grocery packer, the thrill of being a grown-up and receiving our own money is all we need.

As time goes on, our career starts to have a little more definition: it becomes a name with form and structure. 'Manager, analyst, consultant' we answer primly to the question of livelihood. No matter what stage in our careers, we find ourselves jammed into the in-between place, the dreaded grey zone where things on the whole are just fine except for that distant rumbling we experience from time to time. Sitting in a meeting, going to work on the train, we start to wonder if there isn't something more out there. The older we get, the more we wonder – what are we waiting for? Or indeed, we even wonder if there is anything out there. 'Oh well' many of us say, 'good is good enough.'

The whole business of careers can be so deadly serious and earnest. How about the idea of playing around? Why don't we just have some fun and experiment? Imagine the surprise going to a party and sidling up to someone who tells you with a straight face that he is a Chinese comedian.

On becoming a Chinese comic

The Chinese comic Dashan has been performing for the past few years on national Chinese television to audiences of millions. He performs xiangsheng, a centuries old Chinese performance genre based on puns, double entendres, and word games. Strange? Only if you realize Dashan started out life as Mark Rowswell, an ordinary Caucasian from Toronto, Canada.

It seems unbelievable but Mark stumbled into being the most famous foreign comedian in China as the result of his ability to have an open state of mind. Having flunked French in high school, Mark wanted to find another language. He chose Chinese for two reasons. One, he was working with a Chinese pal and thought it would be a lark. Two, he thought China was opening up for business, and it might just come in handy. So, he went on to study Chinese at the University of Toronto, with no real career in mind. No problem since Mark is one of those people who doesn't force a link between university and a career. So off he went to study something interesting and fun. Four years later, armed with a scholarship, he then set off to study at Beijing University. At the time it so happened that BTV, Beijing television, was hunting around for a foreigner to co-host a major television special. Being curious, he thought it would be interesting to see how a special is made and went along to volunteer. Little did he know that it was the beginning of an exciting and successful career. The show was done and broadcast simultaneously on 17 regional TV stations across China. This led to the ultimate invitation to perform in the annual New Year's Eve Special on China Central Television (CCTv.) Mark performed in a 30-minute skit, portraying a workaholic husband named Dashan who comes home late from work once too often to find himself locked out by his wife, who was also played for laughs by a foreigner, a female student from Brazil. They were scripted to have a very funny conversation through the door, all in a slang Beijing dialect.

Dashan was born! He had begun his new career as a foreign comic in China. Then, into Dashan's life walked Jiang Kun, China's premier star of comedy. He took Mark Rowswell under his wing and began to teach him the ancient art form of xiangsheng.

He was later inducted into the revered centuries old society of xiangsheng, the only foreigner ever to be admitted. And all this from a guy who studied Chinese as the result of a chance working relationship in a part-time job held during high school. He does not believe in destiny as fate. He believes in having an open state of mind so that opportunity can take hold.

Sidebar to the story

The key to Mark's success was having the right state of mind about his career. He left himself open to life's possibilities. He did not see school as a hard, cold investment. He did not take a one-step, two-step approach to his life. He chose to study something that was of interest with no really clear view as to where it was all heading. He believes that people should throw preconceptions about good careers and bad careers to the wind and see where they end up.

Are you in the crackle stage in your career?

The following questions should give you a good idea of whether or not you are at the crackle stage:

◆ Are you really doing what you want?

◆ Are you too cynical – talking yourself out of having it all?

◆ Do you know what you'd rather be doing?

- Are you proud of saying what you do for a living?
- Do you know what work makes you really happy?
- Do you worry about expecting too much from your job?

How to fuel that crackling feeling

This crackling state of mind is the feeling of not being quite happy enough. If you're smart, you'll figure out how to use this discontent as fuel for change. You have to work with the restlessness, savour the feeling of something missing, roll it around your head. Give it time and energy. Let go of logic, facts and rationalization. Give in to the feelings of unhappiness. Get beyond the superficial feeling of unhappiness and delve into the specifics of the situation. What is it exactly that you don't like? Is it the routine, is it the work, the industry itself, or is it more personal, the boss or people you work with? What is missing?

Failure to analyze the dissatisfaction can result in making a move that at best is a swap from bad to just as bad or worse. Many times in my own career, I have considered a quick switch, a lame little change for the sake of change without really thinking of what I was changing to or why. Luckily, I have always come to my senses and waited until I was ready for the bigger change, the one that would get at the root of my dissatisfaction, not the one that would be merely a diversion. I remember almost convincing myself how much fun it would be to work as a policy writer for the government. A panel of dull looking but well-intentioned bureaucrats grilled me on the finer points of spending 12 whole months on one boring policy statement. Luckily I came to my senses and got out as fast as I could.

A friend of mine has what looks like a dream job to outsiders for she is in charge of leadership development in a company that is always winning human resource awards. The only problem is she is not sufficiently happy to keep going. She is toying with the idea of opening a bookstore or working in the volunteer sector but is mindful of being a single mother. Right now her fears about money are weighing her down. To help her decide one way or the other, she has to permit herself to dream and envisage possibilities, even though it may seem impossible from where she is sitting today. True as this is, many people find it difficult to grasp the idea that you can have what you want if you dare to dream it. We have so much conditioning built in that says we aren't allowed to have it all. People with children have enormous responsibility that suggests sticking it out is the practical thing to do.

Those of us with parents who lived through a depression, the second world war, or hard economic times tend to believe deep down that one should be grateful for just having a job that pays well. An implicit warning written into our unconscious suggests that seeking work as a form of expression is somehow a frivolity. But times have changed and it is now possible to go after what we want – the opportunity is out there.

My mother, who grew up in England during the second world war, is of a generation that never expected a life defined by what one wanted. Those were the days of sacrifice. Children didn't question going out to get any job to help the family eat. Parents did not sit around the gas or coal fire at night saying 'now Johnny, what's your vision?' Kids didn't sit around the same coal fire saying 'look mummy and daddy, I'm not feeling very fulfilled these days at the munitions factory.' Those of us born after the second world war have generally lived a good life and many of us sit uncomfortably in status quo land wondering and worrying about getting older and not finding our destiny. We are the dream-catchers, the ones who want to bag the ultimate job and find our true calling.

What would you do if you were a millionaire?

The point is you have to work at admitting your dreams. One way to get at your true vision is to ask yourself what you would do if you were a millionaire. Other than lying on a beach sipping margueritas, what kind of work or project would you take on just for the fun of it? This kind of thinking will start to get you close to what you really want to do, not what you think you should do. The pull of a positive image of what you want out of life can help to propel you into a better career, meeting new people and experiencing different environments. The skill is in working hard at developing the picture of what really excites you, what you're really passionate about. It is knowing what work you would do for free.

Stop – letting go

This state of mind is best described as the time in your career when you have let go. You are simply going through the motions. Day after day. Not a lot of passion or emotion in the job. Just a job. Even though you may be very competent and very good, there is no longer any real connection. That loving feeling is long gone. The man with the white board counting down the days until retirement. Your body may be at work but your mind is somewhere else. I am amazed at people who say things like 'I could do my job in my sleep.' As if they are proud of the fact of not being connected and alive. Even when you are angry and have snapped, there is still a lot of energy. Negative emotions are still emotions. At least there is some life left in the career.

When you are in stop mode, you really have stopped caring about the company, about your job or really what happens. It is like driving in your car, getting to your destination but not really remembering how you got there. It is being on automatic pilot. In this state of mind, you are emotionally 'frozen' although you do show up for meetings and everything. It's just your heart's not in it. You probably don't even realize how much you've stopped caring.

Don't get stuck on the pause button.

I've often been involved in big reorganizations where people lose their jobs. This is not easy stuff. Sometimes people lose their jobs as a result of real redundancies and downsizing. Sometimes people lose their jobs because of personality conflicts, nothing to do with logic and facts. But people also lose their jobs when they have been stuck on the pause button for too long in their careers. You would be amazed at how obvious it is within a company who the 'stopped ones' are and when they stopped. These are the people with no real passion any more for what they are doing. And guess who is at the top of the redundancy list? You got it. When people have let go of the passion in their jobs, the enthusiasm for making change and leading initiatives, it is obvious to everyone around them. Interviewing these people can be quite deadly. Being in a room with someone who has stopped caring about their job is stifling. Their negativity can suck the air right out of a room.

Are you in the stop stage in your career?

The following questions should indicate to you whether you have reached this stage in your career:

◆ Do you know what you would do if you were fired today?

◆ Do you take your job for granted?

◆ Are you in control of your next career step or is someone else?

◆ Are you passionate about your job?

◆ Why are you still there?

◆ Do you worry about your career?

People in this state of career mind, sometimes get into whine mode and play the game 'ain't it awful'. They sit around taking shots at everything that is happening and are critical of people who they consider up-and-comers. They're not excited and don't like anyone else who is. This is the dark side of the stop state of mind. Sometimes it is a little cosier: a time when you simply take your job or company for granted.

Like a comfortable armchair, the warm dent envelops your bottom as it always has. There is a feeling of entitlement, a sense that you own the job. It would probably never occur to you to keep your résumé up to date, your network alive and well, because you've just settled in. You in essence have let go of your own career and handed it over to someone else if you are always waiting to see what happens next, if you are outside of the game. This zone is dangerous because it can be a precursor to getting fired.

We can all find ourselves in this state of mind at some point in our career. When we remain for too long in this state of mind, it is almost always dangerous. Someone else will usually take charge of events and force something to happen.

A really good friend of mind ended up in this bad state of mind although he was not aware of it. He worked hard and was very dedicated. Loyal and true blue, he was the ultimate loyal employee. Steady and reliable until of course the day his life fell apart when out of nowhere he was fired. Plunged into chaos, he had to start over. He had not looked at his résumé for 15 years, he was not prepared. He had stopped being active and in charge of his own career. He figured the job would always be there. He had stopped taking care of his own life. He has done a fantastic job of getting back into the job market but it took longer than expected because he wasn't ready.

I have to admit though sometimes getting fired is just that. It has little to do with you. It really could be some corporate despot who takes over and takes an instant dislike to you. I don't want to imply that if you get fired, it's because you deserve it. It's not the getting fired, it's how you handle the getting fired that counts. But back to the state of mind. You should never ever be complacent and if you're smart, you will always be in charge of your own career. Options, always have options. Never give up on life's possibilities.

Many people who are fired or made redundant from their jobs will admit later that it was the best thing that ever happened to them. They concede that without being fired, they would never have found the courage or will to make the big change. Granted there are also some people who never recover from being fired, they languish in the shadow of their former selves.

Imagine firing yourself

What I want you to do is get ready for the experience of being fired even if it will never happen to you. Other than getting fired, how can you create this kind of momentum? Many people are discontent and seem to be waiting around for a fat severance check from their employer so they can run out the door into the arms of their destiny. I keep telling them to forget it. They are too good at what they do to actually get fired, and they would really have to work on becoming poor performers. Getting fired takes too much energy and would be virtually impossible for any decent performer to bring about.

Forget the severance pay and start developing the skills that allow you to achieve the state of being able to master your own destiny.

The joy of letting go

Writer Amy Tan, author of the best-selling book *The Joy Luck Club*, tells a wonderful story about letting go. As a child she grew up expecting to be either a brain surgeon or a concert pianist, largely due, as she humorously says, to her parents' insistence that the brain was the most important organ in the whole body. She recalls secretly wanting to be an artist but being afraid of having no talent. So she dutifully went into pre-medical school until realizing that this was not a workable option, switching to English, going on to do a Master's degree in Linguistics. This caused tremendous friction with her parents. She began teaching and eventually left to join a small communications consulting business. This worked well for a while although she really wanted to move into writing and away from project management. When she told her business partner, he laughed and told her writing was her weakest skill. He told her to stick with project management. At this point, she stood up tall and told him that he had no right to decide, since after all she was a partner. 'No you're not,' he said. 'I never actually signed the papers.' When Amy said the words 'I quit,' he retaliated with 'You're fired.' Either way, the job was over. It didn't matter who had the last word. Amy was out on her own. She began to do business writing, proving her partner wrong, by going on to pursue a fabulously successful career as a freelance business writer, working for Fortune 500 clients such as IBM, Pacific Bell and AT&T.

Eventually she found herself mastering her own destiny and that was to write fiction. Even though she was working 80 hour weeks and had plenty of money rolling in, she began to experiment with fiction writing, somewhat unsuccessfully at first. Her career really evolved when she began writing from her own very personal experience. Hence *The Joy Luck Club*, the story of a first-generation American Chinese girl, which went on to be a bestseller. Her story provides us with a great lesson on the power of movement when we're sent flying though the air due to someone else's push.

snap, crackle or stop

momentum

What's your state of mind today?

How do you really feel about your career? Do you believe in your heart that you are working in an area that fuels your passion? Are you in a place that is allowing you to express your talents? If today was the last day of work in your life, do you think you have done everything you can to make for a rich and fulfilling career?

If the answer is no or maybe, then you need to spend more time thinking about your attitude and state of mind. Maybe you can't up and quit your job. Maybe you'll never get that fat severance payout. Maybe you can't see a way out of today. What you can do, is decide to decide. People who have made fairly dramatic career changes almost always point to that seminal moment when they snapped and said 'enough is enough.'

chapter three
snap

more on today no longer being an option

Two roads diverged in a wood, and I, I took the one less travelled by, and that has made all the difference.

Robert Frost

Snap is the moment of truth when we realize it's time to take a turn in the path of life. It can happen suddenly, even take us by surprise when we least expect it. All we know for sure at the time is that the job is over, finished, the end. We might not be ready to take action but the state of mind is crystal clear. Status quo is simply not an option. People describe this as either a big light bulb clicking on or a screaming monologue going on in your head. Either way, your head and heart are telling you it's over. Learning to work with this state of mind is a powerful way to ensure you stay in charge and control of your own career. Although the situation might be fairly awful and you may be in a flux of not knowing what to do or where to go, at least you know that your mind is made up. You are now open to possibilities.

The most universally loved poem, according to Robert Pinsky, United States poet laureate, is Robert Frost's *The Road Not Taken*. Why is that? Is it because we are fascinated with the idea of change or do we like the fairy tale ending with the suggestion of happiness if only we could figure out the right road. I think we are ultimately fascinated with the idea of crossroads and the delicious possibility of choice. Getting ready to take that first step can only happen when we get our mind in gear to say enough is enough.

I can't take it any more!

Meet Su Grimmer who's learned to accept when she snaps and has to move on. She's done it a few times in her career and is now an expert at accepting the power of her own state of mind. As national account executive for Global Television, she once came back to her office after a horrific negotiation with a client, plopped down in her chair and screamed loudly in her mind 'I can't do this job for one more day.' Snap. Su had just entered the state of no return. No matter what would happen in the months to come, she was now ready to move on even though she didn't know to what. As it turned out, she got a call later that day from a man who was starting up a new television network for children. Having snapped, she not only agreed to meet the guy, she made sure it happened that very day. Su ended up being one of the original architects of the wildly successful YTV – youth television network – and all because she snapped. Yes timing is important but she has learned from that experience to accept her own state of mind.

Nine years later, then vice-president of YTV, she did it again. On a long plane journey back from a conference, she read a book about following your dreams. Snap, she resigned from YTV the very next day. But her mantra to this day is to never let yourself get into a job where your freedom of spirit is curtailed, never let go of the power of making your own choices and taking charge. Above all, never lose your laugh. She believes once you accept that it's over, possibilities will come to you. Before she took the plunge and quit, she had already been preparing for change. She wrote her own vision on a piece of paper and stuck it under her blotter. Every day she would take it out and stare at the words she had written to herself 'where do you want to be in five years?' As president of her own marketing company, Flycatcher communications, she's now in the state of career where she is mastering her own destiny. She's not at her final destination or anything, she continually reinvents herself through work and that suits her just fine.

There are many points in our life where we reach a crossroads. Sometimes, we reach this point as a result of our unhappiness at work, a time in our career when we realize the status quo is no longer an option. The future may be unclear but the present is clearly unacceptable. The difference between those who move on and those who don't is what kind of action you take once you've snapped. Look around your office; I am sure you know people who are hanging on when they are deeply unhappy. They've snapped, they just haven't done anything about it.

Life after snap

There follow two stories about people who snapped: one prayed for it and the other planned for it. Neither one knew what the outcome would be but both have fairy tale endings. We can learn from the power of admission. Both people came to the realization that they just had to get out of their careers and make a change even though neither of them had any idea where it would end. They are special for their ability to take the road less travelled. Think about the power of knowing today is not an option.

Praying for a snap

Meet Lee Wood, or Woody as his friends know him. He ran away from the business of saving souls into plain old business. In one year, he went from making $25,000 a year saving souls as a youth minister in a Christian ministry college in California to a lucrative career selling print and internet advertising at a six-figure salary and climbing. His transformation was virtual – in the sense that he found support from a professional career coach named Marla whom he found on the internet. They have never met in person even though he credits her with his amazing transformation. She credits him with having the insight and guts to admit that his life in the church was over.

Woody had to snap a few times before actually making the leap. He began to do his work on change secretly and silently while continuing to work as youth pastor. He started to read books and articles on change and transition. He logged onto the internet for inspiration. He went to a hypnotist. He began to talk out loud to himself about getting out but naturally he was terrified. Where to start? He didn't like the environment, the people, the job, the rules or the money any longer. His mantra to this day 'any person persuaded against their will doesn't stand a chance at living.' Fourteen years of servitude was a long time. In addition, he liked to body build, a definite forbidden pleasure and one soundly renounced by the church hierarchy. Day after day was measured out while his wife and five children tried to eke out a living on a lean salary of $25,000. He began to ask himself if there wasn't something more to life. The rules were strict. His teenage daughters were not even allowed to wear slacks, and his simple desire to work out and body build was seen as a sin.

One Christmas season, Lee Wood and his family took a one-way trip to Baton Rouge, Louisiana, to visit his father who was dying. His dad had been trying to persuade him for years to make a change but, as Woody put it, he was so far in the box, he couldn't hear. The elder Mr Wood died on Christmas Eve 1997: another snap. The last straw came when the pastor of the church community back in California didn't even call him. There he is and not even one phone call, one card, one kind word. Lee decided on the spot, right there and then, that he was not going back. Although he took a local minister's job to tide him over, he had really snapped and knew the real issue was getting out of the church altogether. He continued to search the internet and read books for inspiration. After connecting with professional coach Marla on the internet, he found the inspiration to make the big change. Little did he know that he would soon be working for a major telecom company selling internet and print advertising.

He is living an extraordinary life today not only as a result of what he is accomplishing but also because of the dramatic changes he has made. He is happy and knows that he has learned the skills necessary for mastering his own destiny. It started with accepting his state of mind that life as a youth minister was over.

Woody has a big vision and is on the path. He has a vision of some day standing on a stage in front of some 80,000 people. He can feel the audience breathing as his eyes sweep across the thousands of faces. The picture is still hazy. He's not quite sure what he is doing on that stage in front of all those people but he believes this is part of his own personal destiny.

Sidebar to Woody's story

Woody's story is a good example of the power of giving in to your emotions – the ability to accept you've snapped, that the current career is over. You don't have to have a clear vision of where you are going, you just have to admit that it is time to move on. It is then critical to cement this idea of it being over. He found it useful to get professional coaching assistance, and coach Marla believes that Woody is one of the most focused people she has ever met. He wasn't only open to coaching, he also did the hard work involved to make the transition from one career to another. He never once asked her to take responsibility for changing his career; he knew he was the one who would have to make it happen.

Figuring out the best career doesn't have to start with quitting the job. Such a process can begin much earlier – at the time when the ending is mentally invoked. Once there is recognition that the status quo is no longer an option, it is only a matter of time before you will have the chance to take action and find an alternative.

Planning for a snap

The second story is about Peter Beyak, a Canadian lawyer from Calgary who found a most unusual career as film producer of the $6,000,000 IMAX production *Extreme*. This IMAX film showcases people who work with 'no rules, no limits and no boundaries'. These are world-class athletes who make danger a part of their lives. The film is in worldwide distribution, has already grossed $21,000,000, and is still going strong.

Peter is an ordinary guy who took the predictable and safe path. A Bachelor of Commerce, followed by a Masters Degree in Business Administration with a definite nudge towards law school by his parents. Since he had no other plans at the time, off he went to write the law entrance examinations with a casual attitude and enough intelligence to get the grades for a ticket to the halls of justice. His first day in law school, Peter snapped to the realization that law was not going to be his passion. He didn't act on it at the time but the rest of his life would come back to that moment even though it took him a while to get it right.

After one year in law school, Peter knew he had to get out and so he left to work at one of the big five Canadian banks. For a kid who had always completed what he set out to do, the word quitter came to mind and eventually gnawed at him enough to force his return to law school for another three years so he could say he did it. He was not pursuing anything like a dream; it was simply a need to finish what he had started. And this he did.

When Peter was doing his articles, he could not stop thinking about the unfortunate fact that law work did not make him feel particularly satisfied. But once again, he did the responsible thing when his parents urged him to try it out for at least five years. Like an apprentice tradesman, he committed to a five-year sentence. It wasn't that he wasn't good at law, it wasn't that he hated law. He even liked the people and the great law firm where he worked but realized that, even after five years, he would only get to move down the hall to an office with 40 more square feet and more of the same work. He could see it all measured out so predictably.

At the five-year mark exactly, Peter quit his law job. There was the inevitable going away party at a local bar where he ran into an old university pal and ski buddy, Jon Long, who was the only person to congratulate him for quitting a job with nothing else in sight. Whereas everyone else had been hounding him with the predictable question 'but what will you do?' This chance meeting with Jon Long gave Peter the opportunity to move into the mastering destiny career state. Jon was a sympathetic character. As a professional accountant, he had found himself on the street during the oil recession in the late eighties and was now pottering around trying to make sports films.

Imagine, at this point Peter Beyak has been out of work approximately one hour. He had got so far as toying around with the idea of going to bartending school, just for the fun of it since one of his friends owned a chain of restaurants called Joey's Tomato. (As you can imagine he was not getting a lot of support for leaving a lucrative law practice to learn how to make the perfect marguerita.) Remember that no one, including Peter, had ever thought he was going to be an IMAX producer. He was just stepping off the path for a look around. It all started when he sat in first-year law school and knew that this was not really going to be the driving inspiration in his life.

Peter agrees to meet Jon for lunch, and this meeting launches the idea of producing independent movies about nature sports – surfing, rock climbing and skiing. They did not then go out and rent cool loft space in downtown Calgary but simply started in a spare room of Jon's apartment with no financing or real plan. Peter hauled his computer and fax machine over and they began to see if there was a possibility of making sports films. Both shared a love for sports and Peter figured his law skills might come in handy. After all, you don't take a lawyer with an MBA and ask him to draw a picture of his vision or sit around brainstorming on a flipchart. He had to tackle the business of film production just like any other case. Facts and logic would have to prevail. A business case had to be built and easy it proved to be. IMAX had been developed by Canadians over a period of 25 years and then sold to US interests who in a few years had plans to open another 100 IMAX theatres. Most of the current IMAX products were beautifully executed documentaries but were not packaged for pure and extreme entertainment, as was their plan.

Everyone needs to find a way to actually get started. For a long time, Peter stayed in the comfort spot of networking, researching and playing with the possibilities before realizing he was in fact going to be an IMAX producer. It was only when his younger brother threatened him with exile if he was not allowed to invest and be part of Peter's dream, that Peter started saying out loud, 'I am making an IMAX film.' This threw down the gauntlet. No turning back or an admission of failure. Real money from his brother virtually guaranteed success from the hardworking, responsible Peter Beyak.

Sidebar to Peter's story

Sitting in law school that first day, surrounded by the other chosen few who had managed to beat the odds and get accepted, it must have felt difficult to accept the sinking feeling that this was not going to turn out exactly the way he had hoped. What we need to learn is the power of admitting the truth to ourselves even when it's not very pretty. Living with emotion not logic – that is the ultimate snap state of mind.

Being good at a job has nothing to do with being happy.

The fact that we are good at a job doesn't mean there is any connection to happiness. Peter was a good lawyer even though he was unhappy. He then took action and made a big leap by quitting a well-paid job, one that society looks on approvingly. There is a delicious irony in the fact that he met his future business partner at his own going away party from the legal profession. He knows that quitting his job was the key to his finding a role called IMAX producer. Another change took place once he began to say to himself 'I am an IMAX producer.' Such a statement helps us to make our own commitment and we begin to feel comfortable with the idea of a new career.

Proud of his product, Peter will soon be out of a job since the series is 'in the can' as they say. Not sure of his next move, Peter isn't worried because he knows what happened last time and besides he knows the alternative would be sitting in the bigger oak-panelled office down the hall from the other lawyers. His one true rule is to be happy. He also has learned the skills and ability to master his own destiny.

Creating two roads for yourself

Until you can admit out loud to someone that today is over, moving on is highly unlikely. The idea of working with unhappiness may sound odd but it does work. Giving in to your secret complaints and concerns can help you snap into the realization that today is over. If you don't get to the breaking point, you'll never move forward in new directions. Getting to this point involves serious self-examination. Before jumping to other options, it is essential to analyze what exactly it is in the present circumstances that you want to retain and what you want to leave behind.

Think about the following. What do you like about your current job that is important to retain? Now make a list of what you want to leave behind:

- What skills do you use today that you want to use in the future?
- What do you do today that you don't want to be doing in the future?
- What part of the job do you want to keep?
- What part of the job do you want to leave behind?
- What is missing from your life? What do you want more of?

In order to find a crossroads for yourself, you may have to seriously examine the path you're on before considering what other possibilities exist. So work with your unhappiness, savour it, roll it around your head and give in to the negative feelings. Only when you've come to the realization in your mind that today is over, can you move onto another path. Even then, you will have to decide how much you want to change and if you're willing to put in the time. It is possible to carry on with the job and find sweet indulgence in your personal life. It comes down to a choice of how you want to live your life.

Sometimes I think we should just forget what we think and deal with how we feel. If we don't feel particularly inspired by our work, imagine that we are not in the right place. Make that restless feeling, that nagging thought that something else is out there, work for you. Explore that tinge of uncertainty and see what you come up with.

As a matter of fact, the power of looking around when you're not deeply unhappy is enormous. Staying ahead of the curve is a recipe for career success. The only way to do this is to be constantly on the lookout for opportunities. Keep up your network, never become complacent.

04

chapter four
crackle

more on being at the crackling stage

If you can you will, if you can't you won't. Either way you're probably right.

Steve Winn, Chairman of Mirage Resorts, Las Vegas, Nevada

The feeling of crackling discontent is like subtle music in the background. Sometimes soft and sometimes very loud. When at full volume, the feeling is scary because of the overwhelming realization that you are meant to be doing something else with your career and life. Or sometimes the feeling is just unsettling, a nagging thought of possible discontent. When at low volume, the job seems pretty good, even great, and you start wondering if you're crazy to be so restless. It is easy to get lulled back into the harmony of it all.

If you are in this category of being relatively happy, not desperately miserable to make a change, then you are in this crackling state of mind. You can go forward and make a change or you can stay where you are. Either way might be exactly right for you. You'll never know unless you try. Risk, by definition, means taking action without knowing the outcome. It's a hard one to deal with. Only when we look backwards do we see how each step made a difference, how our decisions either worked or didn't. Who's to say what is right? The only thing I do know is that we have to make a conscious decision.

One of the major drivers for change is saying I will, not I want to.

I remember the first time I ever completed a career questionnaire. It was based on the great work of Dr Edgar Schein, who had devised a method for determining your ideal career. The theory was based on the idea that individuals are anchored to a certain type of ideal career. I remember how disappointed I was to discover that 'management' and not 'entrepreneur' was my number one anchor. I wanted to redo the questionnaire and fake out the answers to come up with something a little more sexy than corporate management. This was an interesting reaction because I had never really sat down before and thought deeply about being an entrepreneur. What this incident did for me was change my motivation. I began to acquire the will to change my destiny. At the time, I still didn't know how to be an entrepreneur. This event happened in 1985, five years before my own flight from the corporate boardroom in order to open my own consulting practice.

If you can, you will

So the will to change is a significant factor for that time in our lives when we are mildly discontented and wondering. It doesn't mean having to take radical action, quitting your job and starting all over again. One of the best ways to tap into mild discontent is to pursue your passion in your spare time and at weekends. Use your lunch hour to go networking, for example. You can begin to develop alternatives to your day job if you spend your time wisely and work at other possibilities in your spare time. As I've said before, getting to the state of mastering your own destiny takes a lot of focus and hard work on your future. It's not radical nor does it necessarily involve spending extra money. It just involves an investment of your own energy. For example, I am currently on my second book while holding down a demanding career in consulting. I take vacation time off to write, use weekends and the early hours of the morning. Many of us are doing two things at once. Will I ever make writing a full-time career? I don't know yet, but I am positively experimenting.

If finances demand a steady flow of income while working on your talent, then consider putting in the hard time and work during nights and weekends until you can make the second job pay. If you're too busy working to network your next career change, you'll lose out. No job is that important!

Fortunately yours

Rhonda Lashen is the founder of the million-dollar business called Fortunately Yours. She went from being a teacher to running a business that makes personalized fortune cookies. However, she did not quit her job and hang out a sign that said 'open for business' the next day. After college and teaching in a drug and rehab institute for a few years, she realized that teaching was not the calling she had hoped for. So she became open to opportunity knowing that her current job wasn't her ultimate destiny. Then a casual comment by a friend about a gigantic fortune cookie sent as a gift, stuck in Rhonda's mind – at that point only because it seemed a neat gift idea. When she herself went to order one as a gift, she was surprised to hear the company was no longer in business. So here was a crossroad that many of us face all the time. The ones who don't bother to try, sit around sipping wine at parties, regaling their friends with the fortune cookie company's misfortune, dropping the fact that this would make a good business. Nodding and sipping, people drift home and do nothing. Except Rhonda! She started making gigantic fortune cookies in her parents' house, experimenting with manufacturing the right recipe, figuring out how to market and sell them. (By the way, she was doing two other jobs at the time.) A customer then happened to ask if she would do little fortune cookies with personalized messages in them. Being open to possibilities, she said yes rather than tell the guy she only did big cookies. Eventually she was able to quit her two other jobs as her business grew. Quitting outright was never a financial option.

Sidebar to Rhonda's story

Rhonda was not desperate or in a state of angst over her career. She did experience some of the symptoms of being in the career grip. She was losing her passion and enthusiasm for teaching, and had come to the realization that teaching wasn't quite the career she hoped it would be. Being neither happy nor particularly unhappy, she was able to open her mind to other possibilities.

Can you spot the signs?

If you want to tap into that crackling feeling, you have to spend some time thinking about how you feel today. Are you experiencing symptoms of career grip? If so, you're probably experiencing a good dose of career malaise and probably aren't sure where to turn next. The first step is spotting the signs. If these symptoms go on for any length of time, you need to accept that what you are doing is probably not a good fit.

Naturally we experience some of those symptoms every week at work. I am talking about prolonged symptoms of this nature. You may be in more of a rut than you think. So look at this list and see if any of these signs feel familiar.

If you are normally down to earth, practical and focused on the job, do you find yourself:

◆ not paying attention to important details

◆ making stupid mistakes

◆ daydreaming more than usual?

You are ready for a change if you find yourself losing it at work, not able to focus and making silly mistakes. This would be disconcerting to you since you usually keep your head down and do the job at hand, without getting caught up in all of the fluff. If you're daydreaming a lot, it may be time to change. Staring off into space is not something you usually do so it feels weird to be doing this. Pay attention to this experience.

Again, we all experience some of these sensations. When these feelings are prolonged for any amount of time this is when we should be thinking that a cigar is just not a cigar. Trust your instincts and figure out what to do next.

If these are some of the symptoms, you know you are feeling bad about this lack of energy and enthusiasm. You are tending to be quiet these days. This worries you and the people you work with. You are the one who is always coming up with new ideas and opportunities so it bothers you that you have lost your drive. You are losing your identity, not knowing exactly who you are any more. Pay attention, there's something going on. There's a strong possibility that it's time to reinvent your image.

Since you live for doing things right and have low tolerance for people who are less committed than you, it is hard when you yourself begin to coast, doing the minimum and just getting by. Losing your drive for perfection is difficult to accept. There is a sense that no one cares anyway, so why should you? You are questioning why you have been loyal to your job and your company. Pay attention, something is happening. Continuing will be dangerous to your career health.

> If you are predominantly the people type, the one who understands and is sympathetic to how people really feel, do you find yourself:
>
> ◆ not caring as you usually do
>
> ◆ feeling mad and wanting to lash out
>
> ◆ worried about not being supportive?

People come to you with their problems because you have a reputation for helping them through tough spots. You are the kind of person who picks up on people's emotions at work; you know what is going on for people when others don't.

You are the one who always looks out for others so right now it's strange that you just don't have the energy to care about others. In fact, you find yourself getting downright angry most of the time. You feel fed up with others and don't even want to be around them. You feel you are right and they are wrong. You probably want to be alone or feel like running away. Trust your instincts.

So what else might be holding you put?

If you do have a sense that there may be something else out there, but you don't know what or you think your current job is just okay, you are likely to be concerned by the fact that you do not know where to turn or how to get started. Your old worries about money may be coming up again and you probably think you might be stuck at the job so you can pay the bills. You might even be getting fed up at the energy you are having to expend even thinking about changing careers. And besides you keep telling yourself that the money is what's stopping you. Or you may find too much security where you are, especially if working in a big company with lots of opportunity. You may be rationalizing continuity of money with happiness.

So how do you get out of this?

Deal with the money problem head on

Here are some fascinating facts about money that are worth considering. When seminar participants are asked 'how much money would it take to make you happy', the response is always more than I have now by 50–100 per cent.' Whatever the size of their income, people always feel they need more income to make themselves satisfied. Traditional conditioning then is 'more is better.'

We always say we need more money to be happy.

Our relationship to money will have a lot to do with our outlook on career change. Finding work that lives up to our expectations may mean more or less money. You can't do things for money alone: money can't be a goal for career satisfaction. I am not talking about the accepted fact we need money to live. In a recent study, presented at the Academy of Management in Cincinnati, of 900 managers surveyed, nearly 40 per cent said they would junk their jobs if they could afford to. In a similar survey conducted in 1955, only 14 per cent of respondents said they would quit if they could. Interesting times we are living in.

Your money or your life

When people start to push at the idea of your money or your life, tell them you plan on having both thank you very much. It is not an either/or situation. If money really is a barrier to moving forward, then you will have to find ways to get the money thing in control.

You have to decide how much money you want to be making and how much money you need to make. They are two different things. Choosing a career for passion and expression does not mean going from rich to poor. As a matter of fact, I'll bet you it is exactly the opposite. When we do work that is right for us, we're very good at it and that often means money follows.

Being in debt and having no savings is the ultimate albatross that will tie us down to a meaningless job. Fear of moving will be too strong if we are in serious debt. If the financial aspects of a change are too impossible, the first step will be to climb out of the debt ring. Being out of debt doesn't mean being rich – it just means clearing the way to consider possibilities that include a drop in income.

It may mean dipping into retirement savings, taking a loan from anyone – parents, friends, or a bank. (Although banks are notorious for their claims of wanting to help new business owners – they often grind you down so much in the details of an elaborate business plan, that the world has moved on and you're left with nothing. They usually say no in the end to ordinary people.) If you are not prepared to take a loss, then maybe you should not be making the change. It is not that you will lose money when making the change, you just need to have the realistic attitude that you might.

Taking yourself through the money paradox

Provided we have enough to live on, our attitude to money is related to our need for security. So if the kind of career change you are contemplating has the potential to impact on your income, you have to try and suspend your fear.

Being needy when it comes to money is like being desperate for a date – that date never comes when you're desperate. Only when you decide to make a life for yourself does someone pop into your life. If you can develop a healthy detachment to the issue of money, deciding that you will find a way to secure the income you require, you will find what you are truly meant to be doing. You will also find that money comes.

Here are some ways of thinking about money:

◆ Don't think about careers in absolutes: rich or poor – imagine that you will have what you need.

- Think about what you would do if you were rich; now ask why you can't do it right now.
- Imagine what work you would do for free.
- Where do you want to be?

There is no real talking anyone out of the fear of loss of money. It is something you will have to work on. What I do know is that you cannot really ever be successful in your career if you do it for the money alone. It will catch up with you. Anytime I have ever accepted consulting work because I needed the revenue not because it was the right thing, I have always found it exceedingly difficult to get through the project. My heart wasn't in it and, guess what, it shows.

The paradox of letting go

People who have taken risks look lucky in retrospect. At the time, they were just as scared as you and me.

Take my friend Martin Pentony-Woolwich who is hugely successful because of his ability to consider moving down the lifestyle ladder in order to make a change. At one time he was working for a communications company based in the UK that dealt with communications and multimedia business, covering large corporate events, making videos and holding corporate presentations at big company conferences. It was at such events that the company was often asked if they would also handle the conference registration – not too sexy but a practical necessity for conference attendees. Martin was invited to start up the little division and he soon had the venture up and running. However, the company was then sold to a bigger organization, and as they were not interested in this small division they offered Martin a job with the bigger company. He, on the other hand, thought that the conference registration business was viable. In fact, he was surprised at the whole business of what seemed to be a tiny little process in the events business. He was at a crossroads.

They had the guts to step down the lifestyle ladder.

Martin and his wife Lee-Ann lived well. They had a nice big house in Surrey and three children. He could give up this new venture and go back to what he knew how to do or he could make a pitch to buy the division and go it alone. He and Lee-Ann agonized over this dilemma, knowing the risk involved with a new business venture and the fact that they had a family to look after. After debating the pros and cons, they came to a most important conclusion and one that changed their lives: they were prepared to move down in income. The plan was to go ahead with the new business venture but with a shared understanding of being prepared to sell the house and move to a flat or apartment should money get tight. I give them both credit for this decision. I wonder myself whether I would have the guts to make this kind of decision for it is one thing to sit around sipping wine talking about starting a business and the idea of sacrifice, blah blah. It is another thing to do it. So you want to know what happened? He worked hard and was determined to make it successful. Today Martin is sitting on top of a hugely successful business venture. He never had to sell the house – in fact he has just completed an extensive renovation. Yes, they are rich today because of their ability to suspend the need for money at a certain point in time.

Sidebar to Martin's story

The moral of this story isn't 'change your job and you will be rich,' but rather letting go of the need for money often makes the money flow. The real lesson in this story is how important it is to have the courage to take the risks and suspend your fear. Martin mastered his own destiny by empowering himself to take charge and have faith in his own talents. Although he sees it as major luck, it's really about his courage. Most people would have taken the safe and predictable path up the career ladder in the bigger company.

Risk taking

The definition of risk: taking action that could result in loss before knowing the outcome. Later, it looks easy from the rear-view mirror when you see how it worked or didn't. I met someone once who had been offered a chance to buy into the hugely successful Trivial Pursuit game for a nominal fee. Ten investors with a few thousand started the worldwide phenomenon. The guy I met had turned them down. He kept saying 'If only I had known.' Well, then there would be no risk, would there? It isn't the fact that he turned them down; the important thing is to analyze what he would do differently next time. The real issue is whether he thought the idea was a winner in the first place.

Here are some ways to increase your risk-taking ability when it comes to switching careers:

◆ Develop the best-case scenario for your career idea – write it out. What is working about your new choice? What is happening?

◆ Develop the worst-case scenario – what is the worst that could happen? What can go wrong? Spell this out even in terms of money lost.

◆ Looking at both scenarios – what can you do to avoid the outcomes of the worst-case scenario?

◆ Now rate your overall chances of success:

   1   2   3   4   5   6   7   8   9   10

Analysis

If you rated fewer than five, here is how to increase the chances of success:

◆ Can you do this work on some kind of trial basis?

◆ Can you reverse your decision if it doesn't work out?

◆ Can you do a step or two or do you have to go for the whole nine yards?

◆ Is it fairly close to what you are doing now?

◆ Can you limit the amount of money at risk?

Any opportunity to test out the new line of work is obviously the best bet for minimizing risk. It gives you a chance to see if you can do it, if you love doing it. This can come in the form of a rotation inside a company, a temporary assignment, taking temporary or contract work. All these opportunities help you to get closer to the right kind of work. Can you do this during weekends and nights while working? This is having your cake and eating it even though it is taxing on your personal life and schedule.

Always leave the door open.

Can you reverse the decision if it doesn't work out? Always leave the door open at your current job if you can, just in case. A technology professional I know couldn't pass up on a new opportunity even though he had been working in the IS group of a bank for many years. He lasted all of three days in the new job and was back the next week at his old job, happier than ever. They were happy too since he was a top performer. He managed his exit so gracefully, he was welcomed back with open arms. His greatest risk wasn't leaving; it was deciding to return to his old job. Many people would not have had the courage to accept the mistake. The deeper question is will he try again? I think he will.

Decide what your contingency plan is now should the new opportunity not work out. This is not being a naysayer but rather being intelligent about managing the risk. It is important to have an exit route. It will help you succeed at change. However, make sure moving back is what you want, that you're not doing it for all the wrong reasons.

Is there any way to break down the steps of the change into manageable pieces just like project management? Can you take one year off, and then go back to work? Can you assemble this change into steps and deadlines, so at least you know you are on track?

If the change is in the same line of work as you are currently in, the chances of success are obviously far greater than if you are switching subject areas or careers outright. Many of the people in this book have made dramatic changes and have still been successful. So imagine how you will be decreasing your risk by staying somewhere in the vicinity of the field you are working in now.

It takes 18 months to make any change succeed.

If the change is to something dramatically different than the work you are doing now, how can you plan to minimize the risks? Or, can you put certain limits on the change? I have a rule of thumb: it takes 18 months to see how any venture will work out. Twelve months is generally not long enough to get the whole picture. Even if you are not happy in the new job, try it for 18 months. This is enough time to qualify as a noteworthy contribution to your résumé. It is not a life sentence. Think of it as an apprenticeship to destiny. Get what you can out of the job or assignment and then move on.

For those starting out on a new business venture, limit the amount of money at risk. Try to attract other investors. Don't feel you have to be a lone ranger. Attracting money will be a test of your vision and determination to make the business idea succeed. Alternatively, set limits – I will spend X amount of money and expect to get Y in return by such and such a month. Once you pass these milestones, you have to act. No point sinking good money after bad. There comes a time when you have to call it quits.

People who want to start businesses are always telling me they don't have the money. Sometimes it's true and sometimes it isn't. How much do you need and what choices are you going to make? Spending money on cars, trips or home renovations may be necessary in your mind but what if you spent this money working in your destiny line? That is the kind of sacrifice you may have to make. If you won't, then stop whining about how hard it is. You're obviously not motivated enough.

Motivation

If you are in a state of crackling discontent, it's easy to get lulled into accepting the status quo. Things aren't so bad, are they? No. Go through another week, month or year and see if it gets any better or worse. That's what you say to yourself. That and 'we'll see.' Maybe your life will work out and be fulfilled. I somehow doubt it unless you get motivated enough to explore possibilities.

A neighbour of mine is anxiously waiting for a golden handshake from a global airline. At 40 years old, he is marking time waiting for someone else to control his destiny. He really wants to be working outside in the elements and why not? He grew up on a farm and can't wait to be outdoors. Too bad he doesn't realize he could say adios to the company and get on with his life because I doubt he will ever be let go of. He might not be happy but the problem is he's very good at the job. Customers, staff and management all love his winning attitude. He will have to take control of his own life if he is to change.

Inaction is justified by the idea that destiny is fate, that old preordained thing again. That way you don't have to take responsibility for your own career. People who work for passion don't sit around saying 'I was born to this.'

Look at the following list of words used to describe motivation. Do any of these mean anything to you? Can you fill in the blanks?

Incentive – what do you need to get going on your mission?

Drive – what will drive you to action?

Impetus – what is the one thing you need to get going?

Spur – how will you needle yourself into action?

Confessions and lies

Be truthful with yourself and ask what excuse you use most often for sticking where you are today. I know, I know. The money is pretty good. The job is good, maybe even great sometimes. The people you work with are great. What if you get something else that is not so good? What if you fail? What if the other side is brown not greener? Well, ask yourself what you are going to think if you don't make the change? How are you going to feel if you don't get up the courage to try something different? Not so good.

Don't ask someone to tell you what you should be doing with your life. No one knows but you. You have to be prepared to make your own deep confession about what you have always dreamed of doing. Believe me it's not going to be totally radical for most of us. It's not like I am sitting here thinking 'Boy, I am working as a consultant today, writing in my spare time but I really wish I was a dentist.' Come on. Finding our own destiny is about working in the same vicinity as the past and present for the most part.

You also have to be prepared to confront the fact that what you are doing right now is on the path to your own destiny, that a slight variation on the theme is all that is required. It may mean the same kind of job, different company. Or different job, same company.

I am not asking you to take gigantic leaps across a cavernous floor. But I am asking you to be honest with yourself and take the time to tap into that mild discontent, that simmering thought that something else might be lurking out there. You have to decide how to give yourself the push. But first you have to make a confession to at least one other person. Tell them what you've always dreamed of doing. See what they say? Now see what you think about what they said. Do you care enough to pursue further thoughts or is staying put the right thing for now?

Is destiny in the genes?

Enter Sam Noto. Occupation, public accountant. Father to Christopher, husband to Charlene. Typical middle-class family until dropping the bombshell that he would 'die' if he had to continue being an accountant. So in his early fifties, he returned to school to study his first and only love, art. Except for Charlene and Christopher, the rest of their families have yet to fully understand why a man would give up a high-paying job to paint and sculpt.

Enter son Christopher Noto who is headhunted by one of the major US banks upon graduation. Top executives come into the orientation and inspire the fresh young recruits, like Christopher, by anointing them as the future leadership of the bank. The executives plead with the novices to change the culture, bring good ideas forward, challenge old ideas, get involved and take risks. 'Ah', they all think, 'these banks are serious about change.'

A few years later, Christopher, along with a few others, begins to see through the corporate smudge. Dissatisfaction begins to creep up silently until he gets the chance of a lifetime by being selected from 4,000 applicants for a position in Asia.

Fast forward. He is living in a $2-million bank-paid apartment in Singapore, he has a car and driver. Life is pretty good and his parents are over the moon.

Crackle. The perks are great but the work includes friction with his boss who does not take kindly to feedback or suggestions. Christopher feels he's in over his head leading a systems group. He decides to channel his energy into personal change by paying thousands of dollars of his own money to attend an intensive workshop in Singapore that has as its core 'you do create your own life.' He lets himself start to vision, 'wouldn't it be great to travel to Bali and bring back antiques?'

Meanwhile he decides to move from his Orchard Road apartment into Chinatown and takes a three-story shophouse. Friends are amazed at his artistic and design sense – his affinity with Asian antiquities. He puts price tags on items, even his own bed, as friends beg to have a taste of the treasures he discovers. His unhappiness with banking deepens. You might think his parents would encourage him to fulfill this new dream but they find themselves wondering why he is thinking of tossing it all in. Maybe we don't learn after all! Crackle turns to stop. He quits his job.

Today Christopher Noto owns three antique stores in Singapore, one of them in the recently renovated Raffles hotel, and has just finished building himself a house in Bali. He did not win a lottery and he wants you to know he is not a little rich boy who indulged himself with a hobby in antiques paid for by mummy and daddy. He didn't wait, like his father, until he hit middle age. No, he figured out early on that you do have to take control and make your own life happen.

If you want to turn the crackle into a destiny, spend time and energy thinking about the following:

◆ Understand if you have the drive to change.

◆ Define the work that you find truly meaningful.

◆ Develop a picture of your ideal job even if it already matches up with today's.

◆ Ask yourself what the consequences are for not changing.

◆ Decide what success looks like for you and your career.

chapter five
stop

more on letting go

Being in stop mode is like being frozen, suspended in never-never land, out of time, out of place. I remember being in this state of mind. It was as though I was watching myself at work through a piece of glass. I could look inside and see everyone going through the motions, myself included. Everything seemed in slow motion. Ho hum, another day! It's a feeling of being disconnected. A sense of wanting to and feeling like you have to distance yourself from what you do.

There's no passion left, no sense of excitement about possibilities. It's like being stuck in a vacuum. You aren't even mad anymore, you've gone beyond that. As a matter of fact, there isn't a whole lot of emotion left. There's a big void. Going through the motions, another business plan, another sales conference, another planning session. Maybe you are even coasting on your past glories, living off a reputation made a few years ago.

Before you can learn to fly, you must learn to fall

This is not a state of mind to stay in for very long. Even if you've snapped, you're energized because you know it's only a matter of time before you get going. It's not 'if' you're going to change careers, it's 'when' you're going to change careers, whereas the stop mode leaves you feeling trapped. Stuck in the middle, you're not sure which way to turn. Stay or not? Leave, but go where? Guaranteed, if you stay here for too long, a few things will happen to you. You'll end up:

◆ marginalized – put out to pasture, corporate exile; passed over

◆ fired or made redundant.

Corporate pasture: home of rare and miscellaneous events

The job works like this, 'We'd like you to be our Project Manager of Rare and Miscellaneous Events. When we have one, we'll call you.' Most companies have jobs that are on the margin, make-believe jobs called special projects. Most companies think they are being kind by putting people into these makeshift jobs that are somehow on the fringes. Never mind that, what about you taking charge of your own career. Are you in one of those rare and miscellaneous jobs?

If you go to circus school and learn to work the high wire or trapeze, you are first trained for a fall. How many of us are trained for career failure? It's one thing to get up on the tiny little metal wire and be told to fall into the soft feathery safety net. It's another thing to cope with a state of mind where you have let go but are still there. If you are in stop mode too long, this is precisely what will happen to you.

Fired or made redundant

One creative multinational company coined the phrase 'career review meeting.' It was an invitation you never wanted to receive since the term was synonymous with getting the boot. If you stick with a job where you have little passion or commitment, you may end up landing outside the company door and not knowing how you got there.

A sure-fire way to accelerate change is to get fired.

The ultimate career stress is when someone else has taken control of your life. 'Thank you very much for making the decision for me.' On the other hand, career failure of one kind or another certainly offers the chance of taking a new path. It is the ultimate opportunity to triumph over adversity. Some of us wish we could get fired because we have stopped caring about the job. Getting fired would mean automatic change. No safety net. The ultimate chance to do something different. This would be so much easier than having to take control and actually quit the job ourselves. Leaving a job is especially difficult when it hasn't reached the diabolical stage. Too easy to justify sticking around. There are always one or two things to be grateful for even if you are unhappy as hell.

Train yourself for failure.

The answer is to always be ready for career failure. Not one day should go by when you are not thinking about what else you could or should be doing. Getting ready and being prepared will make you lucky and cushion you against failure. Make a habit of thinking about what you would do if you were suddenly fired. Train yourself to generate options for finding a way to make money and pursue your passion. There is no one big blinding dream that will come to you, rather the more you prepare to stop what you are doing, the easier it will be. You need to invest in your dream to be prepared when an opportunity presents itself. If you haven't spent time working out your next career step, you may miss the opportunity completely. Do you have enough qualifications? If not, better get going.

Tall, dark and handy

This is the story of an amazing man who, in an astonishing three weeks, went from being homeless to being interviewed on American national television about his handyman franchise called Rent-a-Husband. Today, Kaile Warren runs a multimillion-dollar business and has just received a hefty six-figure advance for writing *The Official Rent-A-Husband Guide To a Safe Problem-Free Home*. He has big plans for transforming the $50 billion home improvement business in the USA and restoring dignity to a profession that has lost its lustre over the years. He's got a regular stint as the 'home improvement correspondent' on the CBS *Saturday Early Show* and has made the rounds of the American television talk circuit stopping by to chat with people like Oprah Winfrey. How did he do it? Well, he got stopped and emotionally suspended in his tracks mid-way through a successful career.

Kaile was living in an abandoned warehouse with a piece of plywood as a door. He owned four possessions: one beat-up van, a sofa, one mattress and a desk. A car accident had left him unable to work in construction so he lost his house, brand new truck and, worse of all, his wife left him. He had an epiphany one night when a rat ran across the warehouse floor. Tears ran down his face, as he wondered how the heck a high-school graduate from a middle-class family had sunk so low. He had the feeling of being suspended outside of himself. He did some construction work to get by but even that wasn't working out. That day his friend and boss told Kaile how concerned he was about Kaile's work ethic. He felt Kaile had lost his desire and passion, that his usual high standards were just not there anymore and that he would have to let him go.

Crying, he told himself that he couldn't take it any more and pledged to himself that he would get out of his rut. That night he woke up at 3 a.m. with three words running clear and crisp through his mind, 'rent-a-husband'. He decided right there and then that he would make this a business by renting himself out to do odd jobs around the house. He figured the idea was a winner since his whole life had been an apprenticeship to handyman work. His mother had worked in construction and he had been around building sites and material all his life. He knew from being in self-help divorce groups that women were in despair not only for losing their husbands but for the stress and frustration of trying to keep the house together and running.

He got up the next morning and went to buy a roll of electrical tape. He applied the three words 'Rent-a-Husband' to the van. The next week he went in search of an attorney to incorporate the business. He went through four attorneys until one said 'yes'. The others all looked down their long noses and basically told him in so many words 'look sonny, ideas are a dime a dozen. You need money to make a business work. So run along and don't get any big ideas in your head'. The fifth attorney thought it was a good idea. Kaile handed over $100 and he was in business. Driving home one night, an 'off the beat' reporter stopped him at a gas station and asked what Rent-a-Husband was all about. After an interview in Kaile's warehouse, the reporter did a story and Kaile was in business. Three weeks later he was interviewed on the popular Maury Povich show, and thus launched a multimillion-dollar business with a promotional line 'tall, dark and handy'.

▶

So how can we learn from this kind of fall from grace without actually falling? You can't plan on getting fired or physically stopped but you can plan on quitting. (You could try to get fired but it's not worth the energy and besides why ruin your reputation?) Taking the plunge and quitting takes courage, especially without knowing where you are going to next. So we all know that intellectually it makes sense to just stop. We know it would provide us with that big opportunity we've been waiting for, yet many of us get stuck, afraid to strike out and just do it. What gets in the way?

Money would be a big one for most of us. Also, the fear of not being sure if we have what it takes to pursue our dream. Finally, we always wonder if this is the right time, if there might not be another time. But how do we ever know when the opportunity is right? Well we don't. Timing is everything.

Timing

When potential clients turn me down for consulting work, the most polite form of rejection consists of letting me down gently with the explanation that 'I'm really interested, it's just not the right timing.'

Indeed, timing is often given as the reason for rejection. Ask yourself if you are in this camp, what will have changed next year to make the timing different? Timing isn't always a form of resistance, sometimes it is just timing. Just make sure it isn't really resistance deep down.

If you have dependants and a partner not able to support a drop in money, for example, then it might not be the right time. The question is, what are you going to do to make the timing better? How can you work on your talent, develop the skills and contacts needed to help you get ahead even though you may have to stay put for now in your current job?

A friend of mine had been working as a manager in the government for 20 years. During one job in her career, she managed to find her true passion, organizing huge events and conferences. As a single mother, she had promised to wait until her two sons finished school before pursuing her dream of opening her own events business. Then her mum just passed away, but before she died, she told her daughter to realize her dream. Guess what, she decided to go for it even though she had to swallow her pride and accept financial help from her dad. After being on her own for exactly three weeks, she was ecstatic. She wondered why she hadn't done it earlier. She credits her parents' support.

If you can't stop, you won't, but don't blame your parents

Think about what your parents had in mind for you when you were growing up. What did they expect of you? The bottom line is to look backwards in a dispassionate manner as if you were reading the headlines of a newspaper. Leave motive and emotion behind for a moment and think about what kind of calling you were originally directed towards.

Growing up in the 1950s, and perhaps due to being in the Catholic school system where nuns were kind and intelligent but lacked any knowledge of the outside world, my own career planning was a simple affair. Girls like me were given three choices: nurse, teacher or secretary. Because I hated gore and couldn't look at anybody's cuts and bruises without swallowing a little hard, nursing was ruled out. Since secretarial school came in the form of attending a convent academy run with military precision down to white gloves and proper etiquette befitting the role, this left teaching. I believe the boys were offered teaching, trade school or engineering. Not a lot to go on, all careers considered.

Any class will experience difficulties in finding destiny.

The facts of one's class and upbringing provide the basic script. The trick is in making your class work for you. If you're not serious about finding your calling then parents and upbringing become a convenient excuse for not going anywhere. In fact, for each class the challenges will be different, not harder or easier. Those born in the poorer or lower middle classes will most definitely believe in their hearts and minds that rich kids can pursue their passion more easily. Rich kids will look at the poorer and lower middle classes and think how easy it would be to find a better destiny when you've got nothing to lose. Anyone with parents who lived through the depression will know that expectations then were plain and simple, to get a good secure paying job. Expectations did not centre around fulfilment and personal desires. It is harder for children of depression parents to accept the idea that it is not only possible to find one's passion but, more importantly, it is acceptable to do so.

If you come from a family that has expectations different from your own, you have a lot of work to do. If your expectations differ greatly from those of your parents, you have to develop strong resilience and learn to be assertive. It takes a lot of self-confidence to pursue something different. So you have to be sure you really want to take a different path.

Bill Gates, one of the wealthiest men in the world and founder of Microsoft, the gigantic software company, admits his parents had expectations for him. He came from an upper middle-class background and was clearly expected to go to Harvard as a matter of form. And go he did, until the fateful day he had to call home and say the words no parents ever want to hear 'I'm dropping out of Harvard.' He did leave to write a computer program for a man who thought the program was already written. Since Bill had a lot of catching up to do, Harvard had to go.

Know where you came from: what you need to let go of

What kind of expectations did your parents provide regarding your career? What did they value in terms of careers? Based on that, what kind of expectations did you have for yourself growing up? What careers did you fantasize about? It is interesting looking back and remembering what you thought about in the early days. Fill in the blanks. Stand back and consider the implications for you in finding your ultimate expression.

If I looked at the following chart and applied it to my own set of expectations, I would write that my parents wanted me to get a job as an executive secretary. They thought I would go to a place called 'The Mother House', a convent institution dedicated to turning out young ladies as top quality secretaries. My own career expectations had narrowed to teaching. What I really wanted to do though was go into theatre arts. My parents dissuaded me with a lot of sighing and warnings about the theatre being no place for a young girl, that it was a hard life, a life with no money. There were also a lot of veiled threats about the 'dangerous lifestyle'.

Your parents' career expectations	Your own career expectations	What you really wanted to do
Secretarial school	Teaching Business Psychology	Theatre arts

Well it's useful to return to early expectations and consider what you used to think you wanted. Some of us have moved on while others will find interesting threads to pick up and start working with again. The practicalities of life may have intervened in the period between childhood and today but early hobbies and interests have a way of telling us where our passion and talents lie.

Hobbies often tell us where our passion lies.

I am lucky to be working as a management consultant. It is not too difficult to imagine why I have so much fun at the job. It involves an element of teaching in that our consulting practice is based on helping clients be better informed than when we started. In essence, our mission is to teach our clients how to fish so they can feed themselves when we're not around. Also, a lot of my work involves public speaking and presentations and although the main objective is to inform, the second one is to entertain. Funny how my work is an intersection of two earlier interests!

What about you – what do you need to rediscover?

I think you will find this exercise interesting. Fill in the chart below and see what your past has to do with your present.

Think about what expectations your parents had of your career. Were they different from yours? What did you expect versus what you really wanted? Maybe they were the same thing. When I think of expectations, I think of what we realistically thought we would end up doing, not necessarily what we dreamed of doing.

Your parents' expectations	Your own career expctations	What you really wanted to do

When it actually came down to making my choice at college, I chose business school at the last minute. Why? Because I fell into the idea of taking a subject that I thought would be practical rather than one where my interests really lay. I knew I was in trouble when, bored with the accounting course, I found myself trying to argue the irrationality of the debit and credit system with my professor. After a year, I decided to switch to psychology. The Dean of the Business School looked down his nose though his tiny reading specs and congratulated me a bit too heartily. I could hear his echoes of goodbye and good luck as I retreated down the college corridors. Much later I went to university and studied English Literature. Why? Because I finally got smart and studied what I loved.

Pick your own dreams.

I used to work as an academic advisor in the college system in Montreal. This experience provided me with a unique insight into the motivations of students and how parents either help or hinder the situation. It was a privileged experience and offered me the chance to learn several lessons. It is no cliché to say that many a parent foists their own unfulfilled dreams onto their children. I had students crying in my office saying they couldn't possibly become a doctor, that they were failing science and didn't know how to tell their parents. Suicides on campus are a very real thing.

One student was failing pre-medicine badly. His father roared into the registrar's office one day with his son and proceeded to yell and launch into a vicious tirade aimed at the assistants and the registrar about the utter incompetence of the college. He said his son was still waiting for a transcript after two semesters. He demanded to see a transcript right there and then. It was obvious that the son had not shown dad his bad marks. The registrar waited until the man had finished venting his anger and told him that the college could not hand out the son's marks directly, that he would have to ask his own son for them. It was like watching a sad movie. Imagine being so terrified that you find yourself cornered, and having lied for so long you finally have your sorry story exposed in front of an audience. Clearly, studying medicine was his parents' idea, not his own.

Think back on your early choices and remember what subjects inspired you. If returning to school is a part of your future destiny, forget trying to make bets on what will be of value and what won't.

You are of value and you have to make sure you do things to add to your own value, not what someone else expects of you.

Other people in our network who can help us to let go

Although we may have left behind expectations from our parents about what we study and what we do for a living, a lot of our motivation to change can be helped or hindered by the people around us today. Our partners, spouses, children, sisters, brothers and friends may influence our own motives to change. If we are surrounded by people who have fairly narrow expectations about work, namely, that a good paying job is the be all and end all, it is going to be hard to let go. If our network is filled with high flyers, powerful, accomplished people, it may be hard to live in their shadow. It may be hard to want a different kind of career or life.

When our support network expects the same as we do – work that is meaningful and fulfilling – we are lucky. When their expectations differ from ours, it takes personal will power to overcome this and make our own way in life.

Who are the top 5–7 influencers in your life today? What do they want and expect of you when it comes to your work and career?

Think about how the expectations are either similar to your own views or different. If they are quite different, you have two choices. Either change your own mind or change theirs. You have to make sure the latter is worth the energy. If you want to enrol family and friends into your own personal vision for change, you must make sure you are absolutely serious. When you assert yourself and tell people with great conviction that you believe you need to change jobs and find a different outlet for expression, they will take you more seriously. If you are ready to be talked out of a change, you aren't ready for the change.

People don't take us seriously when we are not really motivated ourselves.

Once you have made up your mind, you have to negotiate for support. It might be emotional, financial or concrete assistance. You

name of influencer	Their expectations	How do they differ from yours? What is the same?
1.		
2.		
3.		
4.		
5.		
6.		
7.		

might need someone to switch their schedule, or home and childcare duties. It might require someone else to change shifts in their own job to accommodate a change for you. Or you might just need someone to provide you with psychological support. Whatever it is, it can be worth the time enrolling your network. It will help with your motivation.

Even though you are the one to make it happen, getting the network behind you is essential. They can't do it for you but they can help you do it. If your friends have low-level expectations, watch out.

◆ An airline attendant who switched from full-time to part-time duties so she could train as a teacher found her colleagues less than motivational. Some were jealous that she was taking charge of her life and found ways to complain about her schedule requests. They would tell her stories about the difficulties teachers face. She learned to keep her head down and cultivated new friends, ones that applauded her move. By the way, she graduated top of her class and this after leaving school ten years earlier. The airline is now in the midst of lay-offs. She doesn't care as she is happily teaching at this very moment.

Your parents and friends can either help or hinder your state of mind when it comes to pursuing your passion. In the end, you will have to make the choice. It's worth spending time reflecting on your past and considering how it shapes your choices today.

When the conditioning is 'passion over money'

Richard Craze is living his dream working as a full-time writer. He spent 19 years working with a regular salary as a general manager and as a finance manager before he found a way to write full-time. You might not know him but he has written over 50 books. Funny and irreverent, Richard tells a story about when he was writing a book on Chinese herbal medicine. One day he was sitting around, drinking a Polish beer called Felkstrone. The Chinese consider restlessness a disease so he wrote into his book a prescription of felkstrone root for curing restlessness. He reckoned there could be no better cure for restless people than having to spend the rest of their life searching for a root that didn't exist. With a wicked sense of humour like this, it's no wonder he can make a living using his imagination and ability to write.

Richard grew up in England in an atmosphere that promoted creativity over getting a job and making money. He describes his mother as a British Joan Crawford, theatrical and inspiring. He was taught 'you must never get a proper job,' and that you're not doing anything worthwhile if you are not creating or writing something. Theatre, painting, art, all acceptable pursuits! His mother helped Richard succeed in finding his destiny by teaching him to always have an opinion and to always speak out on subjects even if he was wrong. What this did for Richard was create an outwardly confident manner that enabled him to succeed at a few careers before making writing his full-time job. Not a lot of money growing up and not a lot of concern about money. He still feels this today, saying he does not want to be or care about being a millionaire; he is happy writing and pottering, as he puts it. To understand where and how he got started, let's go back in time.

He got a job as a croupier in a casino so he could write in the daytime but ended up rising through the ranks to general manager supervising 80 people. He says he got hooked on regular money and soon found himself married with children and locked into a mortgage. Add to this, the horror of his brothers and sisters who all went into some form of the arts. One day he woke up and asked himself what the hell he was doing! At least during his 15 years at the casino, he had continued writing fiction. No book was ever published although he did get a few short stories published without payment.

The time soon came when Richard decided he had to get out. He spotted an advertisement in the newspaper for a financial manager of a student union at Bristol Polytechnic. They didn't want a traditional accountant because they were dealing with major theft issues and working in a casino meant Richard had lots of experience when it came to the business of cash and security. Voilà, he got the job and went to work as financial manager with a staff of three, armed the first morning with the book *All You Ever Wanted to Learn about Bookkeeping*. He stayed four years.

Along the way he came into contact with a communications editor who was leaving to become an agent. Ha, he thought, 'This is my chance', and he called up after sending along samples of his writing. She suggested meeting for lunch where she told him his writing was good but pointed out that she was only in the business of non-fiction. 'Too bad', he thought with a sinking feeling, 'but at least the lunch was good'. Then, as he was leaving her office, she asked quite casually if he knew anyone who could write a book on graphology. He turned around and instantly said without a flinch, 'I can'. Getting in the car afterwards, his partner asked, 'What do you know about graphology?' He quipped, 'Not much but I have a book on it somewhere at home'. He had demonstrated one of the most important aspects of being open to opportunity – you have to try and do even if you don't really know what you are doing.

Are you able to get to the stage of mastering your own destiny?

You are probably sitting there wondering if you have what it takes to find more passion in your career. If you are sceptical, you discount the stories and think it is a one in a million chance. If you are optimistic, then you're interested in knowing what it takes and how to increase your chances of finding the next career move that will get you closer and travelling in the right direction.

So, let's look at what it takes. See where you fit in and what you can do to up the potential of finding the right career for you.

chapter six
where are you in your career?

don't run away from what you want, run to it

If a wild dog runs at you, call for it. Think about your career fearlessly. Don't run away from what you want, run to it.

Mastering destiny is that state in your career when you know you are working in the right vicinity. It is being passionate about what you do for a living. Imagine someone on vacation sitting on a deckchair overlooking a gorgeous beach, reading something clearly enjoyable. Looking closely, the onlooker spies a dull looking report filled with tables and numbers. When we enjoy what we do, we are consumed. Sometimes we try too hard to figure out what we should be doing. Mastering destiny is finding work that we love to do. The father of one of my friends was a judge and she can always remember him bent over reading through long complex proceedings and loving every word. The law was his passion. He didn't want to read the latest bestseller on his vacation, he wanted to immerse himself in the topic he loved more than anything.

There are four states in the destiny map. Many of us will go through all these states in our working career. Can you remember your first paying job? Believe it or not, I was thrilled to work summers as a chambermaid in a hotel. For a girl who hated housework and had a high tolerance for mess, my parents were amazed at my excitement over bedmaking, washing baths and room cleaning. For me, it had nothing to do with the work, I was just focused on the little brown pay packet. I'm just glad I was able to move on. Some of us may get stuck. Not everyone can get to the mastering destiny state but most of us want to.

If you are interested in completing an inventory to assist you, go to Appendix 1 of this book or log on to **www.yourmomentum.com** and complete it to determine where you are today. It will take you about 20 minutes.

It is advisable to have completed this inventory before reading further.

Where are you now?

So, what's your state of mind when it comes to your career? Snap, crackle or stop? Is there someplace else you'd rather be? Have you reached that point where you know your job is over, that you've just got to move on? Imagine it as a screaming urge to get out of the status quo. A desire to run out of the office yelling at the top of your lungs 'I can't take it anymore.'

Or is it just a crackling feeling of discontentment? A place where you're not fed up enough to jump but you've got a nagging feeling that something else might be out there. Are you at that point where the career is okay, pretty good all things considered? Wow, that is so inspiring. Listen to yourself. Now ask yourself what you would rather be doing with your life.

Or maybe you are stuck on the stop button, biding time. A state where the concept of passion and expression at work is just that, a concept. Do you feel like the world is passing by? Do you think you could do your job in your sleep? Are you connected to what you're doing? Now ask yourself if this is any fun. Don't you have more to do with your life?

At what stage in your career are you today? Do you see your job as just a way to make money, as a way to get ahead in the world, buy the car, and be part of the club? Are you in it for the learning or are you lucky enough to be in that place where the work is you, it's the ultimate definition of all you stand for, what you love to do? A place where time flies and you feel completely absorbed in your work. No deep longing for another kind of job – there's nowhere else you'd rather be.

Mastering invention 'Working for learning' I am experimenting with my talent My job is making me restless I want to take more risks I am trying to overcome fear I am overwhelmed by options I am trying to change I am not sure who I want to be	**Mastering destiny** 'Working for passion' I exploit my talents My job is making me happy I take risks I feel empowered I am doing the right thing I am not fearful about change I am doing what I want to be
Mastering convention 'Working my way up' I use my talents My job is getting me somewhere I plan my risks I am independent I value my potential I don't think I need to change I know what I want to be	**Mastering institution** 'Working for a living' I don't use my talents enough My job is something of a necessity I am afraid to take risks I am dependent I undervalue my potential I am afraid to change I don't know what I can be

Mastering institution

When mastering institution, we are in a stage of our career where the job is basically a practical necessity. Work in and money out the other side. We are pretty happy because we don't expect the job to fulfil us in any deep and meaningful way. It is a time of trying to please others more than ourselves, a time for doing what is right. The job offers us an opportunity to make friends and develop relationships. We tend to be seen as someone who doesn't rock the boat, who is friendly with everyone. We assess the job for how it fits into our life – does it have the right hours, is it in the right location, is it the right place? This state of career, although comforting, often makes us feel relatively tied down with few options. It feels more like survival than anything. It is a stage where we tend not to have a strong identity with our career. We see ourselves separately from what we do for a living.

Mastering convention

When mastering convention, we are in a stage of our career where the career is very important. It is a time for major achievement. We are guided by the ability to move up, to achieve advancement. We want and like the opportunity to move up the social ladder, acquiring possessions on the way. The focus is independence; planning carefully how best to spend our energy, who and what to spend it on. In this career state, we tend to cultivate relationships for what they can do for us. We think of career change in analytical terms, deciding what the next move will be. During this stage, we may take jobs that stretch our talent and intellect but we tend to avoid deep personal change. We think we are saving that for later. It is a time for amassing wealth and material things. It is a time when our 'at work' and 'at home' personalities are often quite separate. This is because we are developing a strong identity and brand in relation to who we are in our careers.

Mastering invention

When mastering invention, we are in a stage of our career where we are guided in our career choices by what we can learn rather than what money or title we can get. We question our whole life including how work fits in (or doesn't). Our career is governed by learning, rather than where the job is on the career ladder. We are trying to learn about who we are more than the work itself. It is a time for cultivating diverse relationships and friends in order to broaden the learning. In this state, there is a tendency for us to scatter our energy. We generate too many options and possibilities; we have too much on our plate. We often find it difficult to get beyond the thinking stage and into action. We have many ideas but may not find the energy or time to actually do anything about them. It is a time when we are developing an identity around what we learn, not what we are doing. We are trying to find a new identity and brand for ourselves.

snap, crackle or stop

momentum

Mastering destiny

Mastering destiny is a stage of our career where career choices are guided by our need for expression. We don't just think about possibilities, we act on them. It is a time of feeling empowered and courageous about taking the next step even when we don't know where it will lead. We are happy and constantly reinventing what we do. We live for what we do. This state in our career is one where we are completely self-motivated and require no one else to prod us into working. It is a time when we have come to trust our talents, when we know our strengths and weaknesses better than anyone. The identity at work and play is the same. There is knowledge that we would be spending our last day at work doing what we are doing for a living. It is a time of constant energy directed towards our passion. We are what we do. We feel lucky for being able to work in our field.

So do we move around?

Absolutely, we do. Some of it is a function of circumstance. Take actors, for example. Many go into acting for the sheer passion and in effect master their own destiny early on. James Kirsch, ex-Broadway actor from New York, sang and danced his heart out in shows by Anthony Newley such as 'Stop the World I Want to Get Off'. Today he works for a computer company, hoover.com and in essence is mastering convention later in his life. He is glad to have mastered his destiny early on. 'If you don't do what you want, you'll always be dissatisfied.'

Martha Stewart, food icon of the twentieth century, worked as a stockbroker until she turned her hobby into a career. Now she sits at the helm of an enterprise devoted to 'foodies' who pay big bucks for the latest in good taste and charm. She is working at her passion and getting paid to have fun. As she says, 'I get up in the morning knowing how much fun I'll have today decorating a wedding cake or picking herbs.' Similarly, the musician Seal was a fully fledged architect before pursuing what he calls his 'life as a human being', a life that has purpose, a life as a very accomplished musician. Michael Creighton, author of Jurassic Park, is a qualified medical doctor. He went to medical school to make a living and then discovered how to make his passion his career.

World-class athletes often master their destiny early on and then wind back into more conventional careers that may not offer as much as their early passion. World Cup ski champion Ken Read says many of his peers fail the career grade by not preparing to change before their bodies give out. He knows some ex-hockey players who are pumping gas – stuck in 'institution'. They never spent time on their future when they were riding high. Ken for one has turned his talents towards television and he now anchors a successful business show.

Jean Auel turned out four bestsellers starting at the age of 40. She doesn't see herself as a phenomenon but rather as a successful mother, business woman and student who went back and did her MBA before she began writing. She demonstrates the characteristics of mastering destiny: she is empowered and knows how to exploit her many talents.

Richard Branson quit school at 16. His headmaster said, 'You'll either go to prison or become a millionaire.' He found passion by starting a magazine, and only became an entrepreneur to support the magazine; the rest speaks for itself. He had no fear, he just took the risk and plunged right in.

Leo Klus was a brilliant consultant who left a lucrative career to pursue spirituality. He got fed up with enjoying what he calls the money pipe and took a chance to go and study at a seminary college. His restlessness finally got him moving to pursue what he feels is fulfilling and to find his passion for life's work.

Steven Chasens started out as a marine scientist and worked in research for the pure learning of it. He then took the conventional route and made piles of money in real estate. At one point he woke up and realized something was missing. Today he works as a successful acupuncturist and is passionate about his work. His advice is to focus on the journey not the end state: 'Once you decide you have to change, the opportunity will present itself.'

So yes, it's all about movement, but first you have to spend time thinking and getting a feel for where you are today.

More on mastering institution

During this state, you are working in a job that probably isn't stretching your potential or forcing you to grow. As a matter of fact, the job might be pitched just under your capacity and even beneath your qualifications. The job is probably comforting and you are probably good at mastering it, without too much effort on your part. You play by the rules and expect your employer to value your loyalty and dedication. You tend to take care of others before you take care of your own needs.

You are probably like a friend of mine who is very capable only he undervalues his own potential. He works in stores, not that there is anything wrong with this, but he is far more capable and overeducated for the job. He has to work on accepting that he has value that needs to be recognized.

You set your sights below your ability.

In this career state, you prefer not to be part of the action but to watch others. You tend to avoid overly challenging situations and will stay in jobs long after they've been mastered.

You prefer to just keep the job as a job and avoid getting involved in office politics. You notice other people getting ahead and are often relieved it isn't you. On other occasions, you see people being promoted over you and wonder why this is so. You do your job and you probably do it very well. You want the world to think that is enough.

In this state, you would likely turn down a promotion if you saw any risk at all; better to stay in a job that is regular and predictable. Risk is also often equated with conflict. Taking a job as supervisor could mean having to exercise discipline, and this could, in turn, cause conflict so you reckon it's better to stay put at the employee level. Outsiders look at you and wonder how you can stand being in the same job, the same place. You keep telling them and yourself that you are happy. You challenge them with lines like 'you think you have to get ahead to be happy?'

If you have been in this phase for a few years, you will have a hard time moving unless something dramatic happens. People have often found that a breakdown or change in personal relationships is the main factor for getting shaken out of the status quo.

You haven't learned to expect fulfillment from your job and that would be fine if you were just starting out in the job market. The problem lies when you are in the middle of your career and still in the state of mastering institution. Money is a necessity but since you tend to undervalue your own potential, it's quite possible you could and should be making more money. It's a time when your identity is quite detached from your actual job – you don't want to identify yourself all that much with what you do for a living.

A woman I know had been loyal to her employer for many years, doing essentially the same job. She loved routine, took the same vacations at the same time, did the same work year in and year out. When fired, she became desperate for any kind of job and immediately began to lower her expectations in relation to salary and position, undervaluing her potential before even getting started. Needless to say, she now has another job that puts her right back in the mastering institution phase. It is beneath her potential but it does pay the bills. She had a chance to move into another career state but chose to stay put.

More on mastering convention

During this state of career, you are shoring up your potential and using it to compete in the world. It's a time of feeling worldly, confident in your understanding of the career game and how to get ahead. You see the positive aspects of getting ahead and value the money and social standing that comes with the job. It is a time when you are comfortable asserting yourself and taking care of your own personal interests. It is a time when external trappings are part of the process: big office, lots of perks, money to buy toys and be part of the right club. It is a time for collecting things, buying into society and amassing possessions. It is a time to focus on getting ahead and advancing as much as you can. Above all, a time when your identity is very much defined by what you do for a living.

This stage in your career is a time of self-interest and self-focus. Looking out for number one! You prize independence and the ability to go out on a limb. You are trying to control the next steps. You seek out contacts and relationships in your network for a purpose. You learn what you want and then move on. You are trying to figure out the rules of the career game and how to play them to your advantage. It is a time of classic climbing of the career ladder, being in a job where you are working hard to make a difference, building up your career chits. You value your potential and may be in a job that does not quite live up to your expectations.

If your company cannot live up to your ambition, move on.

During this stage you are willing to take work risks but not personal risks. It is not a particularly introspective time; you are focused on external change, finding the right place to live, finding the right place to work, and not so much on deep personal change. You feel you have to accomplish something, make a mark, do the job, prove your worth in society. If you are ambitious, it is most likely you will have to plan a series of moves to get to where you want. This is a stage in your career where you often have to make sacrifices to get ahead. That could mean accepting an international posting and will most definitely mean working long hours.

Possibly, you are focused on paying the mortgage and think you'll get a life some time later. It doesn't mean you are just sitting there, oblivious to everything around you, but you subdue your feelings of dissatisfaction in order to get ahead. You accept the rules of engagement in the firm, even if it means adhering to the rules. You see this as part of the game.

If you want out of convention, it is because you are beginning sometimes to experience a void, to have a feeling that you are missing something. You don't like to focus on this too much – it makes you uncomfortable to confront true feelings of inadequacy.

If you are in this career state, you are really thrown if asked to change your personal behaviour in a fundamental way. You have a strength of looking out for yourself but it can also be a weakness since you can often be unaware of the impact you have on others. You tend to rely on your tried and tested methods for getting work done, landing a deal, completing an assignment, etc. Your focus is on your strengths but you often fail to be alert to your own weaknesses.

Your life is not in balance. You either spend not enough time at work because your hobbies and outside interests keep getting in the way or you spend way too much time at work, ignoring an outside life and family. You never feel really satisfied either place; one always seems to be taking away from the other. You consciously limit your energy in both places, never really letting go and devoting all your energy to your job or your life.

More on mastering invention

Mastering invention is the phase in your life where there are more questions than answers. A vague feeling of knowing something else is out there but you're not sure what it is. People see you as constantly being on a quest, of trying to find yourself. You probably joke about not knowing what you want to be when you grow up, only you're quite serious.

You think too much: start acting.

If anything, it is a time of too much scattered energy, trying to do too many things, not focused sufficiently in a few narrow areas. Restlessness must be channelled into a few key actions that are directed and focused. This is a stage in your career when you take work for what you can learn not what it can do for you. The need for learning is a constant in this phase. You may be better at thinking of possibilities than doing them, however. You tend to spread yourself too thin, trying to be everything to everybody. You could learn from masters of convention here because they look out for themselves and are more conscious of limiting their energy.

Because you work so well collaboratively, you may sometimes take on too much, forgetting what is on your personal plate. There is a tendency to broaden out any project because of your insatiable desire for learning.

You believe in looking to yourself for answers and may be too hard on yourself at times. The inability to move, to make the right change, seen as a flaw! It is important to have friends and family involved in what you do. You talk about your work out of sheer enjoyment, not to impress or brag.

It is a time when you are likely to look more confident about your career than you really are. People don't realize how difficult it is for you to make changes, because you make it look easy.

Your thirst for knowledge is insatiable. You're in a state where you tend to fill your life with too many activities, finding little time for yourself. If anything, you overextend yourself and find yourself loaded down at work and at home. Since you always take responsibility for situations, you add this burden to your load knowing that you are the only one who will be able to do anything to improve the situation.

You confront your dissatisfaction but often get overwhelmed with options, knowing there are many things you could be, or should be doing, but not sure which one fits the bill. Mastering invention is a state of restlessness. Sometimes you are gripped with fear as to whether you will ever be able to make the big leap, to what you don't know. Wondering if there isn't some other work out there with your name on it; a yearning for fuller expression. If you are at this stage, you know that the only way you will be able to move forward is through very direct action and commitment. You have to select a path and take it. Not to worry, if it doesn't work out, you will move on.

More on mastering destiny

Mastering destiny is a career state characterized by the idea of you and the work being one. It is a state of feeling enormously empowered, of finding work a place for expression and passion. A time when the job is really well matched up with your talents and aspirations. If you are in this state, you would do this work whether you got paid or not. I don't mean you shun money and what it can buy, I mean that the work is so important you will find time and even your own money to get it done. Mastering destiny is a state in anyone's career, be it teaching, accounting, technology, or marketing where there is 100 per cent passion for the job. It is obvious to everyone that you are in the right job. You fit it like a glove.

Take the gang of Microsoft millionaires, who could retire but choose instead to work because of their passion and expression. There are teachers, mining engineers, researchers, engineers and analysts who are mastering destiny. No longer restless, but content to work in their chosen area and, by the way, very very good at what they do.

The difference between mastering invention and mastering destiny is the fact that you are no longer thinking about change, you are bringing about change. Peter Beyak, the lawyer who became an IMAX film producer (see Chapter 3), had been on the quest for some time even thinking, at one point, of becoming a bartender. Once he quit the job, hauled his computer over to his friend's house and began to focus on the question 'what is possible', he had moved into the mastering destiny phase.

This state in your career holds very little fear. Not knowing what is next is seen as inevitable. There is an ability to operate from a deep sense of intuition, knowing when to move on and pursue new avenues. The rules of career are the ones you invent. You know the answers to destiny lie within yourself. It is a time of being internally directed – you look to yourself and figure out how to get what you want and need. You accept the principle that you might have to take a short-term hit for long-term results. It is a time where you have great interpersonal insight, you know what makes you tick, and you know your shortcomings and strengths. This honesty allows you to constantly reinvent what you do and how you do it.

You've learned to let go and change when your instincts tell you it's time.

In this state, you know you are working in your chosen field. You are happy to be doing what you do and pour your whole energy into this expression. To outsiders you may be described as a workaholic but remember that personal and work life is converged so it would be a mistake to feel sorry for you. Life is blended. Work is fun. Life is fun. You are used to people telling you that you're lucky and, to a large extent, you feel lucky. Deeper down though you know that you have worked hard at defining your own future. You've always known when it is time to move on even before others figure it out.

Finally, even if you are already working in a place that you can say is truly fulfilling and where you feel you can express the best of your talents, you will know that you will always have to re-examine and re-evaluate your life to make sure it still keeps fitting. You know that destiny is not one destination and don't feel you have arrived in your final resting place or anything like that. You expect change and, even though you may be well rewarded for the work you do, you realize money is not the driver, expression is. You will constantly need to seek outlets for stretching your potential.

So where are you and where would you rather be?

So some of you are probably in combination: institution/convention or convention/invention. This just means you are in transition between two states and are at a time when you are actively figuring out your next move. The next chapter provides practical steps for moving on from each state.

chapter seven
where would you rather be?

snap, crackle or stop

momentum

how can you move on?

If only changing careers was as easy as getting to Kansas. In the land of career Oz, we could just click our heels like Dorothy and end up in the right place. A lot of people haven't discovered their Kansas yet and are wondering how to figure it out. To make that change, you first have to figure out where you are and then you have to think. That's right, just think.

After the thought comes one step – not huge gigantic leaps and death-defying actions but one step that will take you closer. There's no way to get anywhere different other than to pick up your body and do something with it. You cannot lead from your seat.

Think Rachael, think!

Knowing that a change is needed and knowing what kind of change that needs to be are two different things. Many people are still troubled over coming to terms with what they want. Although it is tempting to just yell, 'think, think', this is obviously not very helpful. It reminds me of the time when a group of us were playing Trivial Pursuit, a game based originally on North American trivia. So when Rachael, a newly landed Canadian immigrant, was given a question about some American sitcom from the 1960s, she naturally looked blank. Her teammates kept yelling 'think Rachael, think', not realizing how ridiculous and culturally impossible it was for her to come up with an answer. I know that some of you feel this way about changing careers. Just the other day, a client of mine said he was ready for change all right, if only he knew what. I was sorely tempted to yell 'just think Michael, think!'

It takes deep thought and fearless imagination.

Even if you know for sure you want to change, 'the what' is a rather more complicated affair. The process of answering this question is central to making change. Unfortunately it is a complicated question. An aboriginal tradition for helping young men come of age is to have them go alone into the wilderness for a couple of days. The silence and trauma of being alone and self-reliant is instrumental to evolving into adulthood. If we could create this kind of wilderness trek for ourselves, it would provide us with the opportunity to just think. We would have a chance to use our imagination.

No one can tell you what to do or be. No one can define the ideal career for you. You have to find the answer for yourself. The answer is within you. You have to think about what is deep down inside of you: you have to develop self-awareness. If this makes you run screaming and yelling, come back. I'm not talking about lighting a candle and chanting career mantras, it's a little more practical than that. Let's start thinking then about your career state and what you can do about moving on.

Moving from institution

The challenge of getting out of this state involves working on your confidence and valuing your own potential. You have to accept the fact that you can make money and do work that is fulfilling – the two goals are not in opposition. You will also need allies and supporters who can help you get out of your situation.

You can get a job that better uses your talents if you work at it. You'll probably make more money too. First you have to change your expectations. If you've been doing jobs that are below your capability, then you need to work on changing your image. Like it or not, the image you have of yourself is based a lot on what you do for a living. There's likely not a lot of passion for what you're working at now, so go and get some passion. Figure out what you care about and what you're good at. Now tell yourself you can find work that fits into that picture.

You may have to accept short-term pain for long-term gain. To get to where you want may mean a return to school, a need to upgrade your qualifications. You probably don't want to hear this. I know all the stories about cab drivers with advanced degrees too. I also know people with education who are making it work for them, thank you very much. This is not a prescription, just a suggestion. The fact is you may not have the right qualifications to get to where you want.

The following is a list of 12 practical steps you can follow in order to make the move from institution:

◆ Work on defining your strengths and skills: do a new résumé that represents the job you want, not the job you have.

◆ Look hard and long at your qualifications: do you have enough education?

◆ Scan the classified ads and circle the jobs you really want.

◆ Change your routine – do something for yourself for a change.

◆ Talk to your boss about what other roles might be possible.

◆ Cultivate relationships with people mastering invention and destiny, try to understand how they got there.

◆ Work on imagining being fired: what would you do?

◆ Interview five new people for job ideas.

◆ Take a course outside of the comfort zone, the further away the better.

◆ Get a rotation inside the company, a temporary assignment to see what other work feels like.

◆ Volunteer to work on a project team.

◆ Seek professional career coaching.

The bottom line is taking just one step. You don't have to change your whole life, you just have to get started on the path. One of the biggest problems you have is with the money thing. Don't ignore this but think carefully about how much you need and what you need it for.

Or perhaps this will confirm that you are okay with where you are. Maybe you will find other outlets for expression in your life. If so, then stop worrying.

The only thing stopping me is money. Liar, liar, pants on fire!

We all have to eat and have a roof over our heads. But if you just keep sitting there saying there is no way out of the money thing, there will be no way out. If you cannot take the risk, just accept the fact that money is an irrefutable barrier and stop agonizing. If you want to quit working and pursue alternatives, make sure you are totally committed. If you are serious, then you will find a way to get the money you need to live on. Don't believe it for one minute when you tell yourself that it's because of the money you can't find a fulfilling career. Chant the words after me 'liar, liar, pants on fire!' The money argument is what we call the presenting problem in consulting. Beware of dealing with this issue on the surface. You have to look deeply and examine how you can deal with the need for making money while pursuing alternatives.

Fear of being poor is the favourite barrier to change trotted out and laid on the table for all the world to see. Sigh. Sigh. People say 'Yes, I could find a great career if I won the lottery or inherited a lot of money.' 'I would like to try something else but you know I have a family to look after, otherwise of course I would.' 'I'd like to change but gee the money is so good where I am, it sure would be hard to find somewhere else.' 'Oh,' says the lawyer, 'I'd love to go into marketing but I just can't afford to.' 'I'd really like to sell my art,' says the analyst, 'but I just can't walk away from the money.' 'Maybe when my pension pays out,' says the corporate executive, 'I'll go into consulting.' Sad that money becomes the number one barrier to moving forward.

It is too easy to whine. Tomorrow won't get any better than today if you don't do something to get out of the money rut. If it means working and going to school at night, you'll have to see if you're that committed. Think of it this way – you're going to be working anyway, so why not make more money and have fun at what you're doing at the same time?

For better or worse, for richer for poorer

The problem of money can be a big wedge even in a good relationship. If one person is going to stop working, the other one has to pick up the load. If you are in a relationship where the other person does not support your own driving need for self-expression, you are going to have to work at getting their support. Again, you have to make sure you are serious and committed, it's easy to get talked out of change when we want to be.

Most of us can't get from here to there in one fell swoop. It takes time to work on the alternative career. People have dependants, children, financial burdens that need to be taken care of. Finding a great career is not about chucking everything in and running away. You might have to work on your destiny while continuing to work: the two are not incompatible. Little steps can still get you there. For example international experience is probably one of the greatest assets you could have but this will obviously require support from your partner.

If you are considering giving up your regular income and starting your own business, you should plan on putting aside enough money to ride out any bad times for at least 12 months. Remember you can always get another job, there is a safety net. If you have to stay working until you get this cushion, do it. It may be that you really can't afford this or are not able to put any savings at risk, in which case you will need to consider how to ensure a steady paying job can still be a passionate one, where you feel your talents and skills are being put to the test every day.

There's no question, however, that a flat-out stop will help propel you towards the possibilities of destiny. Stopping work is the ultimate insecurity. Naked we stand, no former title, no community, no connection. My husband and I both quit corporate careers in 1990 and got out of our mastering convention phase. The plan was to travel and then figure out a way to survive without steady paying corporate jobs. It was actually exhilarating for two people used to buying things on a whim. Beyond no spending, we also had to sell our house to give us the cushion of money we required to travel for a few months.

We spent two years getting ready by going on a diet of no spending.

Quitting a job works. For anyone wanting to make the transition from corporate to self-employment, it is almost a necessity for shaking off the requirement of regular money. Time away gives one the opportunity to begin shaping a new identity. It helps to drive you forward, especially when money gets tight. After seven months, money was running low, so we both came back and each of us opened our own business. One of the big triggers for both of us getting out of convention had been to ask ourselves what we would do if we won a million dollars. Part of the answer was travelling abroad for a year and moving to Vancouver Island, on the west coast of Canada. We then began to ask the deeper question 'So what's stopping us from doing that now?' 'Oh,' we gulped, 'nothing but us.'

Moving from convention

One of the challenges of breaking out of convention is learning how to question better. Ask yourself if things aren't working out, what changes you need to make. Force yourself to examine your own shortcomings. Spend time thinking about who you ask advice from, now go and ask the same questions of someone completely different. See what they answer. You will need to spend some time examining your own motivations in your career. It would also be helpful to get an outsider's perspective on your career and opportunities. Read books that you would never usually pick up. Force yourself out of the accepted theory that you have to get ahead. Think about having more fun instead.

You don't have to quit your job to get started, although kicking the corporate habit would be ideal. You just have to choose. For you, a good start might mean a leave of absence or working at something else while holding down a job. If you took the opportunity to seek work that is meaningful, rather than simply being a good position, you would be happier.

If you have dreamed of living someplace else in the world, then this is the time to check it out. A forced move can help you to achieve more balance in your life. If not, use your vacations and time off to explore different parts of your personality. If you still want to work on getting ahead and staying in convention, you'll need to tap into some personal growth. Peel the onion and see what's underneath the skin.

On an intellectual level you might recognize how self-defeating it is to work for external motivations and trappings and, being educated, you probably do. It takes hard work to take a long close look at yourself.

The following is a list of 12 practical steps you can follow in order to make the move from convention:

- Consider if you really want to change and how much.
- Invest in your personal growth; work on your interpersonal skills.
- Ask colleagues for feedback on your style.
- Seek coaching assistance from someone you admire.
- Take time to think and reflect about what is important to you.
- Go away; take a leave of absence; get off the treadmill.
- Spend a month where you don't buy anything, see how you feel.
- Think back to your early interests, what were you passionate about?
- Think about having a million dollars with a guarantee of no failure, what would you really do with your life?
- Figure out how to make a living from your hobbies.
- Practice being selfless; help others at work just for the sake of it.
- If work is more energizing than your personal life, work on getting a life.

Changing your routine is probably one of the best ways to shake yourself out of the comfort zone of convention. Spend more time on diverse interests. Stop being obsessed with your job. If you can manage to get off the treadmill, it will change your life.

Learning to live without the corporate trappings and structure is often one of the most empowering things you can do for yourself. If you can get your company to give you a leave of absence, go for it. You'll be amazed at what it does for your inspiration. Introduce some space into your life before it is too late.

Getting stuck too long in convention can have unintended effects. What follows is a true story and a vivid example of what happens when you take the mastering convention stage to the outer limits. It often takes dramatic events to jolt you out of one state and into another. It can be particularly difficult during convention to let go of the trappings and the seduction of an all-consuming career. You probably know someone just like this.

The man who fell from grace

A deal maker by training, Paul managed to rack up a whopping six acquisitions as executive vice-president in charge of Mergers and Acquisitions for a financial company. Jetting all over the place, fine wines and dining, a seat in the inner circle of the corporate world, Paul worked hard and made good deals. His idea of down time had turned into one half day on Sundays. He wasn't doing very well at learning how to be idle (or even relax). The concept of balancing work and family life is still just a concept in hard corporate circles. Working at a frenetic pace, lots of overseas travel, and 15-hour days is par for the course for any ambitious executive. Incentive trips to sunny locations are part of the reward system.

Then one summer, Paul and his fellow executives were invited to a junket at the CEO's sunny ocean-front house in Florida. A treat for all the great deals that had been made. These trips were not voluntary, the silver tray and invitation is proffered without the slightest hint of it being an option. No, the fun is scheduled just like any other corporate meeting and so Paul felt compelled to go even though he wanted to stay home with his family. His wife understandably urged him to go, pointing out that he really should and as he always had done in the past it would look funny to decline now.

Off he went as the reluctant tourist but decided to come back a day early for his wife's birthday. He had bought her a very expensive set of pearls. He sailed home with the precious gift and presented it proudly to his wife. She undid the wrapping and opened the sleek velvet box to find a row of exquisite pearls nestled in the satin folds. Closing the box softly and purposefully, she handed the box back saying pointedly, 'I don't like pearls and as a matter of fact, I don't like you.'

▶

Stunned and feeling like someone had punched him, Paul swallowed hard knowing in that moment that something had snapped. He was being catapulted into the land of bitterness and regret. He knew he had a big problem and that no amount of talking it through was going to solve this one, no dinner out at a great restaurant was going to sooth this turmoil. His life changed right there and then in a matter of 60 seconds.

She went on to say that he had not been there for her or their two boys for years, that he had spent his life working and working some more. When he sincerely pointed out that he had been doing it all for them, so they would all live a comfortable life, his wife stared coolly at him and pointedly rejected his argument saying he was doing it for himself, plain and simple. True enough, he had been relentlessly climbing the ladder in the pursuit of wealth. He had been so focused on himself and his own goals he had not even bothered to notice his partner and two boys. Any notice he did give them was distracted time at best.

After the pearls, Paul bitterly realized that his wife meant business. A few weeks later, he handed in his resignation to incredulous stares and a round of plea bargaining from the CEO and other executives who would not accept his resignation until they had plied him with offers of even more money and perks. For Paul it came down to his job or his marriage. He chose his marriage but it didn't choose him. So what happened? Paul has been asking himself this over and over as he has spent the last few months in major contemplation. First and foremost, he agrees with his wife's critical assessment that life with him was not much fun.

He told it this way. Imagine sitting at a dinner party with a small group of people. Someone is telling a story when another person says 'Oh that reminds me of something. Once upon a time, there was a pig and a chicken.' Paul recalls lasting for maybe a minute at tops before lurching forward with 'but what's the bottom line, does the pig die or not?' The point being quite simply that his personal life was just like his business life – everything had to have a quick point, a bottom line. No time for niceties. No time for listening. He found it hard to see any value in just sitting and talking with no one to influence, sell to, get something from, etc.

After months of reflection, he calls the event a gift in his career. He wishes he could do it over again and get it right this time. He knew he had to get out of the corporate environment that had created him. He took a few months off and is back working again, although for a much smaller company. By the way, his wife did not agree to reconciliation. He is now contemplating a return to school to become an architect.

Moving from invention

Mastering invention can be a really fun phase in your career. Granted, there are more questions than answers. But in this career state, we are genuinely toying with other ideas of how to have a career and live our life. It is a time when we secretly wish to get fired just so we will be forced to take action.

At this stage, you are already on the quest and thinking, dreaming about what else you could do with your life. As a matter of fact, if you have made a habit of working your career this way, you are already pretty good at change and are aware of the need to make changes. It isn't as though you haven't done it before. You have always lived your work life by knowing when it is time to move on. Although you are afraid, you manage for the most part to keep the fear in check and keep moving forward.

Your energy is no doubt scattered between a wide and diverse range of interests. You will have to learn to focus on a narrower range of areas where you can dedicate your energy and mind more constructively.

The challenge is to commit yourself to action. You probably know what it is you have to do. You have to develop the courage to act and focus your energies in one direction.

The following is a list of 12 practical steps you can follow in order to make the move from invention:

- Get rid of one activity and responsibility in your life.
- Work on finding an outlet for your talent while holding down a job.
- Find yourself more time so you can focus your energy into fewer things.
- Engage your partner and family into helping you make the change.
- Work on your vision: what do you really want to be doing?
- Create deadlines and milestones for the change.
- Create your own apprenticeship in the area you want to work in.
- Write out a plan – what are the three things you want to accomplish and by when?
- Think about when you lose track of time – you are getting close to 'fulfilling' work.
- Keep a mental or physical record of what makes you most dissatisfied at work.
- Narrow your options down.
- Shore up your resources so you can make the change whenever you want.

Many people who are in this career state find that setting an age or a time limit in the same role, by which point they will move on, is really helpful. Going to school, learning, channelling the energy in a more focused way, are all good ways to get moving. The key to moving into mastering destiny lies in action, plain and simple. When you take your idea for a new career, or business, and actually start doing it and stop talking about it, you'll be where you want to be.

Set that deadline and stick to it.

Staying in destiny

This is a phase you want to stay in. The way to do it is to keep trusting in yourself even when you hit rough spots. You know you are in the right car when it comes to your career; you may have to change lanes, have some repairs done or shift directions but essentially you know you're in the right car. It might mean a change in location, working with different people but the change would generally fit into the overall landscape of the kind of work you are doing right now.

Because this is a phase in your career where you trust your own intuition and often act on a deeply instinctual level rather than applying pure logic, you generally know when it's time to move on. There is comfort in accepting the fact that this project, this job, is no longer providing the fulfillment and joy it once did. And you will take the necessary steps to move on. Your talent lies in knowing yourself and being able to commit yourself to action. Discontent is channelled into work. Indeed, feelings of anxiety are often reconciled by throwing yourself into more work or seeking new outlets for expression. This is a constant state of mind, taking events that don't fit in and giving them new meaning.

You may find that you have to take time out to recharge your batteries or that your health can't take the pace any longer. This stage in your career is one that is constantly focused on reinvention, fueling energy into your field of passion. It is important to continually expand horizons and consider new platforms and technologies that will help to deepen your passion.

Make sure you take the time to mix with other colleagues in your field, as this is good for your inspiration. Offering to develop and teach others is also an excellent way to refuel your passion and bring new ideas to your work.

Here are 12 practical steps to staying in destiny:

◆ Continue to work hard and focus on what you love.
◆ Expand your knowledge and explore parallel subjects.
◆ Steer clear of people who find you too devoted to your work.
◆ Force yourself to take time off to recharge your batteries.
◆ Help others to develop in your field.
◆ Consider teaching as a way of maintaining momentum.
◆ Consider meditation to keep the focus.

- Work on enjoying diversions.

- Keep up to date in your field; learn from new thinking.

- Become a mentor.

- Do volunteer work that uses your skills; it will rejuvenate you.

- Spend time with retired people in your field; they'll give you perspective.

This career state is one where there is a constant need for reinvention and self-expression. The love of the work is so overwhelming that it is hard for others not to see you as anything other than a crazed work fanatic. To keep your passion alive, you have to promise yourself to take time off, go away, get away from the work in order to refuel. It's easy to end up running on 'empty' after a few years of working at your passion. So make sure you take care of yourself.

So what else is at play if you want to shift quadrants?

There are some other dynamics at play in the process of mastering destiny. They have to do with your attitude. You may be wondering if you have enough courage to do what you are thinking about? Or possibly the real issue is commitment. It may be you have the courage and commitment but are terrified that your talent pool isn't deep enough to succeed in your chosen area. Perhaps you're too risk averse, can't handle the possibility of failure?

chapter eight
the intangible dynamics to mastering destiny

have you got the right attitude?

If you have the right attitude, you'll find your passion. It's getting that mindset going in the right direction. If you believe you'll be successful, you will. If you feel lucky, you will be lucky. It all comes down to working on your attitude. When Kaile Warren got up that morning to buy a roll of electrical tape and put the words 'Rent-a-Husband' on the side of his beat-up old van, he had attitude. So if you are having trouble figuring out what you want or how you'll get it, start working on your attitude before you run out and take action.

Does this dog hunt?

I was once part of an interviewing team that was conducting a search for an executive in the forestry industry. One of the guys on the panel was the owner of his own logging company, down-to-earth and not one to mince words. After we had seen a candidate who had the right skills and qualifications but had come across very poorly in the interview, the logger looked at all of us in our little corporate suits and said in a long drawl, 'This dog don't hunt.' We got it. The candidate just didn't have it, whatever it was. We did eventually find someone who passed the 'this dog definitely hunts' test.

The power of your own thoughts is one of the biggest drivers for change. If you don't have the right attitude, you'll just go through the motions. Here are the ingredients to getting the right attitude:

Attitude = courage

intuition   commitment

risk taking

Courage

Wouldn't it be great if there was something called a bank of courage? A bank where you could sidle up to the friendly courage rep and ask for a neat withdrawal – '600 chits please, this change is a big one and I'll need a lot of reserve.' Even if you are pretty clear about what change you want to make, it will take courage to get from here to there. It's hard to admit that we have to create our own power to make it happen.

I used to think everyone wanted empowerment, a chance to seize control and go for it. Only later did I humbly learn that not everyone wants power. Some are quite content to let others take charge; that way they won't have to be accountable, have the risk of events not turning out the way they planned. Sometimes I feel the same way when it comes to career change, I don't want to be the one responsible, I want someone else to tell me what I should do next, with whom and where. Too bad it has to be me.

If pressed, we can admit deep down what we really want to be doing. If you're saying no to this, you're not ready; or you haven't done enough work yet; or you're not fed up enough. Even if the career dream is impossible, say it out loud.

The problem is self-censorship. You know how we dream for one second and then immediately tell ourselves no, that's crazy, it's impossible. Well let's change all that and start getting obsessed with the idea of having what we want. Let's go over the facts. Do you believe you can get what you want? Do you believe you will be successful?

When headhunters ask applicants what their dream job is, they're serious. So get ready to answer this question. You don't even have to tell anyone right away. The dream might be fuzzy, crazy, unformed. Don't worry about it. Roll with it, try it on for size. Tell at least one other person. Talk it through. Say it out loud. You'll be surprised at how this act begins to shore up your courage.

And it is courage that will help you make the leap. It can be lonely being the one out there on a limb. It takes a fair amount of courage to let go. The next story is one that shows enormous courage in changing careers. The ability to let go enabled someone to find a true passion, one that he did not even know he had.

Courage: strong and free

Maarten Schaddelee went from a 28-year career as a Dutch baker making rolls and cakes to being a world famous sculptor. Breaking away was really tough. After 28 years he found the courage to get away from the only job he had ever known, from his brothers, his mother and father. He wasn't just quitting a job, he was quitting the family. He had to swallow 28 years of hard work in exchange for nothing. Self-imposed exile meant that he had to walk out the family bakery door with nothing but himself.

Maarten is mastering destiny. His sculptures are large and imposing. He works with hard stone and wood materials from the earth, flinty granite and marble from Vancouver Island, polished black and white carrera marble from Italy. These materials take shape in his long, elegant hands to become whales and wonderful abstracts. Whereas bread and cake dough is soft and yielding, a hunk of granite and stone looks sullenly at the artist waiting for something to happen.

Most people are probably thinking he started as a child prodigy but he did not.

Imagine growing up in the Schaddelee household in Victoria, British Columbia. Large square aprons and a light dusting of flour, a warm and spicy environment of baking and brotherhood. As the youngest of four boys, Maarten was the last in line to take up his position. He admits he could never draw very well so his art did not come to him at an early age. He quit school in Grade 9 and went into the bakery full-time. For most of his life then, Maarten was part of a big and inclusive clan where family worked and lived together. Even later as the four brothers got married, their wives too became part of the Dutch bakery team. The family even took holidays together so it was no surprise that customers seemed to linger in the shop wanting to inhale memories of an idealized family along with the smells of spice and cookies wafting through the air, rich iced cakes, rolls and creamy chocolate confections, all nestled in their perfect little white paper cups.

And so life went on for Maarten. While he worked at the bakery, he gorged himself on hobbies during weekends, and his own kids nicknamed him Mr Hobby. At one point, he thought of becoming a cedar canoe builder and built the studio he works in today.

His perfectionism meant that any hobby had to be planned out and executed like a major project management extravaganza. He could not just go and buy a lathe; no, he had to have one custom-built, involving major machinery construction. Not for the average Joe. Did he know then that he was planning for his destiny to come out? After the one canoe, he tried wooden bowls. Eventually he produced his first piece of art, a wooden bas-relief wall-hanging of flowers. He then began painting where he mimicked but improvised on aboriginal motifs. After two short years of drawing and wood carving, Maarten started to carve in the round. He began the difficult subtractive process of sculpting, whereby you have to extract and expel material for the art to take shape. The oddest thing for Maarten was that out of blocks of wood and marble, the whales seemed to materialize and take shape almost of their own free will.

It was as if the whales were breaking out of the stone, as if he knew in every loving detail how to carve them when in fact he had never even studied their physiology. His learning curve was phenomenally quick, and he seemed to work in an innate, instinctual, almost crazy way. In the meantime, he carried on decorating his cakes, but he began to question his existence in the bakery. His three brothers knew he wasn't happy and kept wondering why he had to have all these damned feelings. He was beginning to develop a lot of intrapersonal insight, becoming more courageous about discussing topics like the meaning of his life.

One night he had a near-death experience, what could be described as his final curtain call, exit stage left. Although recovered, he and his wife Nadina took this as an opportunity to leave the bakery, cash their retirement savings and travel the world. Like most people faced with their own mortality, they wanted to do the things they had always wanted to do. Maarten walked out of the little Dutch bakery with not one penny after working there for 28 years day in and day out.

Today, looking around the expansive windows of his studio out onto the ocean and windswept property, the sculpture called *Courage* sits imposingly in its frame. Large white, grey-veined polished carrera marble, the outer circle and inner circle form one piece. Stunningly simple and powerful – a testament to the guts and courage Maarten Schaddelee had to show in order to break out of the spicy bakery and dusty-floured atmosphere into the clean sharp world of sculpture and peace of mind.

Sidebar to Maarten's story

What is so fascinating about Maarten's story is the idea that you have to have the courage to stop first and have faith in discovering the passion. It took the threat of mortality to wake him up, but he did not have the answer before he left. He and his wife had children, they needed to make money to live. To say he has a partner who supports his self-expression is an understatement. Nadina was the one who helped him find the courage. This sculpture sits as a reminder to all who look out from their living room by the sea.

Courage deposits and withdrawals

Some friends are really friends. We're lucky if our partners are friends too. True friends encourage us when we need it and tell us when we're off track too, they are the ones who genuinely care about us and our dreams. Then there are pseudo friends; these are the ones who don't always tell us the way it is. As a matter of fact, they may undermine our dreams by planting seeds of doubt at the wrong time. There are fantastic career counsellors out there in cyberspace or around the corner from where you live. If you think you need an extra boost to get going, don't be shy about soliciting help. Woody who left religion says he never could have done it without the help of a coach (see Chapter 3). When our family and friends question our decisions or thoughts about making a change, they really are trying to be helpful. It's this interaction that tests our own resolve to go for it. If you find yourself getting defensive, it may be just a reflection of your own concerns and anxiety.

Use professionals to up the courage ante.

You have to develop a network of like-minded people, the ones who are also searching and care about the kind of work they do and how it uses their talents. Over time, you will know who to confide in and who not to tell. Confidants can be the biggest help in getting over the hurdle.

Get rid of cynics in your life

You'll leave the cynics in the dust if you work on avoiding them. Just go about your business quietly and before you know it, you'll have made the change and, bingo, they will turn into allies. Cynics are the ones who are the most fearful of change themselves and are therefore generally not supportive at the time of need. After the change, they will often claim to have been supportive. I find this amusing but I have learnt to avoid them in discussions about my future.

Cynical people don't have your best interests at heart, they want you to be as miserable as they are. So don't include them in your conversations about deep-seated dreams and desires. They'll sneer and make you feel stupid. It will set you back.

If you can be discouraged, you should be discouraged.

Some of us may find it better not to talk to people at all. This is not the case for extroverts who get inspired by thinking out loud: they actually think with their 'tongue'. Introverts, on the other hand, get their inspiration from reflection and may find quiet solitude the best way of getting rid of cynical and worrisome thoughts. It is a test of commitment. Quincy Jones, music impresario, says his piano teacher taught him an invaluable lesson and that was if you can be discouraged, you should be.

Commitment versus involvement

Imagine a pig and a chicken are walking down the road. The chicken turns to the pig and says, 'How about getting some bacon and eggs for breakfast?' The pig turns to the chicken and says, 'Oh great, bacon and eggs. For you, this is involvement, for me it's a total commitment.'

Are you honestly committed?

Are you just involved in thinking about the future or are you committed to the idea of finding your passion. Everyone fills their day. That is not the issue, even for people who sit around like a couch potato watching television. Most working people put in a long hard week of work. The issue is working hard at your talent and feeling good about what you do. Lots of people work hard at their jobs – but do they do the work to make the change?

Commitment is about taking responsibility, not blaming or envying others. People keep asking me how I find time to write a book while jetting all over the place doing my management consulting job. I tell them it comes down to spending my time during weekends and early mornings, on airplanes and in hotel rooms working on the book rather than doing something else. It does come down to the choices we make. I choose to write because I enjoy the chance to express myself.

You have to decide if you are really committed enough to reach your vision. It may mean doing two jobs at once. It may mean school while working. If you aren't prepared to put the hard work into it, just sit back and stop agonizing about another kind of career. Not everyone is committed enough to make it happen.

People who are mastering their destiny are notoriously hardworking and focused about their future. They are not sitting around waiting, their actions are making it happen. They experiment even if they fail. Go and ask people who are living the kind of life you want. Find out if it is luck or commitment.

'Your dream has to be maybe an inch or two bigger than you can manage.'

Maya Angelou

It's easy to talk ourselves out of moving forward. I do it all the time. You can feel hopeless knowing you need to make a move from here to there. At the end of the day, we have to be determined enough to make it happen, even if it involves beating all the odds. No one will knock at your door out of the blue and say here is what you want. People will help you reach your vision if you practise saying it out loud and ask for their support. But not just anybody! Talk to people about what you want and you will find that they give you leads on how to get there. Over time you will collect a network of associates who are supports not cynics of your vision. Avoid the cynics, they will drag you down and tell you it is impossible to get from here to there. Who needs them? They take energy away from your own momentum. You have to believe in yourself and act on the beliefs. You have to stem the fear.

Risk taking – a cultural and personal phenomenon

Canadians, unlike Americans, are not known for being risk takers in business. We are a conservative lot when it comes to career, job security, money, savings and entrepreneurial spirit. Risk aversion is well bred into our culture. It is not a 'go for it' culture where friends and associates applaud bold moves. We're getting better but we're still not there. In the United States, and I know this from working for Levi Strauss and Company, there is a much more open spirit of adventure when it comes to risk taking. When corporate Canadians pack up, quit, leave suddenly to open a business, try a new venture, the general reaction is muted horror. Canadians don't generally respond 'wow, go for it.' Polite questions like 'what will you do if it doesn't work out?' act as a mask for their own fears and envy.

- What is your country's culture when it comes to risk taking?
- What is your own personal view?

Our ability to take risks in our career is either limited or enhanced by our personal circumstances. We all have a certain conditioning to taking risks that comes with our upbringing, how we've been either rewarded or burned for taking chances in the past. So, what's your attitude to risk? Imagine that someone phoned you and a friend to offer you both the chance to come and work at a brand new start-up venture. You listen and think the idea is clever. Your friend decides to go for it and you decide to stay where you are. Your friend spends a roller-coaster year, at the end of which the company goes broke. What is your reaction to this story?

Who is further along with risk taking? The one who took the risk or the one who didn't? Exactly. Ten points for the one who tried and failed. You cannot develop a tolerance for risk taking unless you experiment. The bigger risk from a career standpoint is not taking the risk at all.

It is important to realize that the biggest risk you can take in life is not uncovering the great gift or passion you might have. You have to follow your own heart and ideas about what you want. If you fail, so what? At least you won't regret it. What could go wrong if you don't take the risk? Ask yourself how it will feel to stay in the status quo? If the answer is 'not so good', then best to move on even if it is to the unknown.

Ultimately, our reluctance to take risks in our career is based on the idea that mediocrity is okay. If you feel average about what you do, then you haven't found what you're supposed to be doing with your talent. One key element to risk taking is our ability to trust our intuition and to sense what we should be doing.

Intuition – that old gut feeling

Intuition is present in everyone, although some people have better developed skills than others. Why is that? They have learned how to reinforce their own intuition by observing how many times their perceptions score over reality. Some people have had intuition bashed out of them. They believe that the world works in lines and tables. When faced with major decisions, they try and quantify the dilemma: pros and cons, minute calculations about impact. Afraid to trust their inner voice, they march along with pen and paper.

When we are in the state of mastering destiny, we have developed our intuitive ability to its highest level. Using this ability to help us with problems and decisions means suspending our dependence on logic and facts taken at face value. It means tapping into deep places and knowing when to make a move, change relationships or work situations – just because it feels right. It is the ability to reinvent a way for us to have maximum expression. To take an analytical approach involving pros and cons would not tell the story. When the Canadian Chinese comic Dashan (see Chapter 2) decided, out of the blue, to take a course in Chinese, he admits to feeling deep down that it would somehow be a good thing: he operated from intuition. I'm sure people at the time thought he was wasting his time because they could find no logical way of connecting taking a language degree with his ultimate destiny as a working comic. And at the time, he didn't even know where it would all end. He just went with his feelings.

When Perween Warsi started making samosas, it was partly as a result of her perception that other people also found supermarket versions tasteless (see Chaper 2). She did not sit down and do a business plan. She did not set out to start a multimillion-dollar food empire. She just trusted her hunch.

There is an old saying in consulting, 'When you feel it, trust it.' I have often been involved in projects where I have developed a feeling of something not quite right, of people trying to undermine the results. Whenever I have ignored the feelings, it has been to my cost. So now, I act on the feelings and if I am wrong, better that than not doing anything at all.

We all come to different crossroads in our career where choices present themselves. Sometimes we just have to rely on those intangible feelings despite the logic. But the key to intuition comes with time. The ability to check out our perceptions with how reality comes out is what hones the skill: highly developed intuition comes with reinforcement. The more we trust our instincts, the more times we are right. The more times we are right, the more we will trust our intuition. Naturally, there is always a risk and a time when we will be wrong. Nine times out of ten we won't be though. Instincts work.

Here are a number of ways of exercising your intuition:

- ◆ Force yourself to make predictions about people and events and keep track of how often you are right.

- ◆ Make a decision based on gut feeling alone with no real facts to back it up; see how it works out.

- ◆ Call someone you suspect can help you with your career; see if you're right.

Intuition is like a muscle, the more exercise it gets, the better it works. Trusting in yourself, trusting in who to contact and knowing who can help you will help propel you towards your goal. When calls seem to come out of the blue, imagine that they have a deep purpose. Be curious, figure out how these contacts can help you.

Putting all the dynamics together

Doing a force field

You can pull together all the intangible dynamics that are either pulling you away from or towards your career destiny by drawing a force field diagram. First draw in arrows that represent forces that are helping propel you towards your dream. Use the length of the arrows to signify weight and importance, so longer arrows represent important drivers, shorter arrows less important drivers. Now draw down arrows that represent the forces preventing you from reaching your goal. Sometimes, the same thing can be both a driver and an inhibitor. Stand back and look at the picture. The idea is to strengthen and bulk up the drivers and, where possible, remove the obstacles. I think you will find this interesting.

Analysis

I had always dreamed of writing a book. My husband had nudged me and cajoled me for years. He kept telling me that since I read so much, I must be able to write. I told him there was no cable in the brain connecting reading and writing, they were two separate activities. Turns out he was right. My desire, motivation and discipline were probably the three most powerful forces. I complete the job when I set my mind to it, but there are a lot of forces pushing me away from the goal.

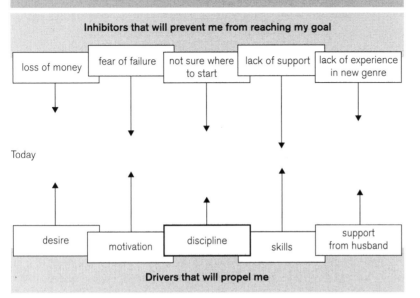

A Force Field   My Vision (where I want to be)

Inhibitors that will prevent me from reaching my goal

| loss of money | fear of failure | not sure where to start | lack of support | lack of experience in new genre |

Today

| desire | motivation | discipline | skills | support from husband |

Drivers that will propel me

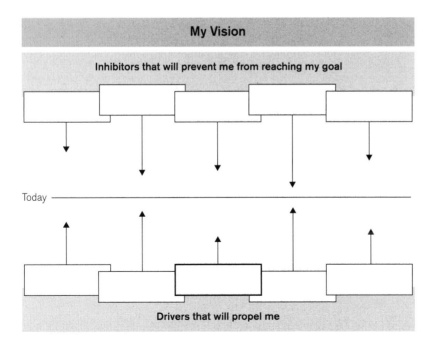

My Vision

Inhibitors that will prevent me from reaching my goal

Today

Drivers that will propel me

Being the owner of a business, how could I take time out to write a book? How could I handle the drop in income to write? What I did was convince my business partner that we should write a business book. It killed two birds with one stone: it legitimized time off from consulting to do the book: and helped me develop the discipline to write. It worked, although it took about a year to get this all together.

So take a piece of paper out and do your own force field analysis. Look closely at what is driving you towards the change and what is holding you back. Try and remove some of the forces that are stopping you while strengthening the ones that will send you forward.

The bottom line on attitude and dynamics

The reality is we have to take charge ourselves and face our own attitude towards change. We all find excuses for not moving forward, many of them to do with friends, spouses, parents and partners. When we have doubts, it is a convenient excuse to blame others. I know when I feel like blaming others for my inability to do what I want with my career, it's time to smarten up and realize that I am accountable. When I find myself in blame mode, I know it's time to recognize it as my problem, not someone else's.

In the movie *Last Night*, people only found out at about five o'clock that the world was ending at midnight on the same day. The movie was amusing for showing how people chose to spend their last few hours on earth; the usual suspects included food, drink and finding old lovers. In our careers, it is interesting to think about how we would spend our last few days if we were forced to stay working. What would you finally do with your career? What is left undone for you? How would you want to spend your time?

What do you need to get started right now?

09

chapter nine
power tools for action

explore the possibilities

The way the world works is all wrong. We should get our pension as soon as we get out of school so we can have the opportunity of exploring and experimenting with as many types of work as possible. Wouldn't it be great if we had ten years to try out all the possibilities? Wouldn't it be fun to turn over as many rocks as possible, kick as many tires as we can while exploring possibilities for our career?

So fight the tendency to settle in too early. Go and experiment. Kick some tyres!

Here are some of the power tools that can help you change career (not everything will fall neatly into an equation that absolutely points out 'where to next', but you'll find some signposts). How do you know what is possible if you don't give it a try? How do you know what you like if you only base your choices on your experience to date?

- Self-assessment: getting to the 'what'.
- Personal vision.
- A reality check.
- Your own apprenticeship: add to your talent pool.
- Action.

First you have to do some serious work on defining your skills, aptitudes and preferences for work. After you have done this, what is your picture or vision? Decide. Where do you want to be? What do you want to be doing? What kind of environment do you prefer: small office, big company, corporate or consulting? When you work on your vision, you need to write it out. That way, you can look at it in a year and see how far you've come along.

Nothing ever gets better as the result of doing nothing.

A reality check is just a good practical way of increasing your knowledge about what is possible. It is going and talking to real people who are doing what you crave to do. Then you need to think about your talent and experience: what kind of apprenticeship can you create that will fatten up your talent? Lastly, it's action you need. Stop sitting there, get up and get going. The more inaction, the worse it gets. Nothing ever gets better by avoiding action, indeed action helps us to stop worrying. People in this book didn't sit around waiting for good fortune to happen. They got motivated. They acted.

Self-assessment: what are the skills you love?

The more you get yourself out there on a limb, making contacts, exploring possibilities, the better you will feel. This is a guarantee. Don't ever let yourself get into the valley of inaction during your career.

There are many resources and tools available to help us explore what kind of work is most fulfilling and most suited to our skills and our personality. Appendix 2 in this book provides you with a list of excellent source tools to help with your analysis. You can find them online through the internet, in your local community and probably even in the local library. They really are worthwhile. If nothing else, such an analysis will at least confirm some of your qualities, and provide explanations if you are feeling deeply unhappy in your career today or even just restless. But you have to make the time. Go on. Get up right now and find out more about these excellent source tools. If you don't, you're not serious enough. Or maybe you're lazier than you think.

No one actually admits to being lazy even if they are.

How well do you really know yourself? These inventories offer the potential for real insight. They will not tell you precisely what to do but they will often point the way. It is a relatively easy thing to do. No real risk in doing this kind of self-analysis but an important action step to get up the courage to make change.

Self-assessment tools

Self-knowledge is one of the most fundamental keys to mastering destiny. It is our ability to understand and accept our personal wishes and preferences, not what is important to society. We have a responsibility to know our own strengths and weaknesses. Sounds logical but many people do not know themselves. If they do, they seem oblivious. If most people knew themselves, we wouldn't have the problems so often encountered during performance appraisals in organizations: difficult people are often surprised to hear that their interpersonal skills aren't quite up to scratch; managers who take all the glory and leave their teams in the dust, feigning shock when informed they are lone rangers. So true self-knowledge is obviously not a common trait. Not enough humans have the capacity to recognize themselves. But we have to work at knowing who we are.

If you don't know, then ask people close to you. They can usually provide insight into your best talents. A friend of mine has a vision of being self-employed. He sees it as the most fantastic possibility for working, and believes that he could do it if only he had the financial means. I don't know. Maybe yes and maybe no. I think he has an idealized picture of self-employment, and he needs to explore further the question of whether he has enough discipline. He has to do more homework to see if he has what it takes. He has to take responsibility for seeing if he can do it.

When we avoid the need for career change, we often blame it on time … next year would be better, or perhaps after one more project, etc. Knowing ourselves means knowing in our heart that when we do this, we are using time as a convenient excuse for not moving forward. Or perhaps, as so many people tell me, they don't really know what they want. There is nothing new in the universe here. I do believe you know, you just haven't done enough work to get to the truth. But if the following skill list helps, go for it.

Skills pool – getting closer to the 'what'

Here is a simple exercise to head you in the right direction. Look at the list and tick off the skills you currently use in your job.

- Solving technical problems
- Working with computers
- Dealing with facts
- Solving mathematical problems
- Resolving conflict
- Influencing
- Dealing with numbers
- Supervising people
- Synthesizing information
- Managing
- Working in teams
- Being creative
- Implementing – seeing things through
- Making decisions
- Working autonomously
- Teaching
- Crisis management
- Counselling
- Having fun
- Working with theories and concepts
- Coaching
- Interpreting data
- Directing people
- Establishing policies and procedures
- Being artistic

- Critiquing
- Mentoring
- Generating ideas and options
- Facilitating
- Writing
- Selling
- Influencing
- Using your imagination
- Initiating projects
- Public speaking
- Entertaining
- Attention to detail
- Reading
- Mechanical skills
- Physical stamina
- Change management
- Negotiating
- Research
- Persuading
- Meeting new people
- Analyzing data

Now look at the list, and decide which skills you are best at and most passionate about. This will give you clues about what kind of talents you need to make sure are present in your future career.

Now paint the ideal role:

I would love a job that enabled me to use the following skills:

_____

_____

_____

_____

_____

_____

- Is it possible to find this out in the market?
- Can you convince someone to bucket a job like this together?
- Who and where might someone want these skills?
- Can you combine paying and volunteer work to see how it feels?

Go one step deeper after looking at these skills, and begin to tap into your secret desires. Move away from logical analysis into dreaming.

Admit to your secret desire

People are constantly frustrated by not knowing what they want to do. I like to push them hard to admit their little secret or fantasy. Everyone has one. Let's face it, the dream is often a variation or extension of what we are doing today but still it is hard to say it out aloud. Why? Because we are afraid of being laughed at or, worse, that we say it and then never do it.

You've heard it all before and you know it is true. You have to take concrete action to make vision work. If your vision is to be at school learning something new, you have to do the searching to find the right course. If your vision is to start your own business, talk to people who already have their own business, people who would be potential customers and find out what they think. If you never find the courage to talk up your own vision, no one will be able to help you. I don't believe in the theory that you should keep your little vision to yourself.

Develop a personal vision

I know that vision works. You might be sitting there and thinking you don't know how to develop one or that it is all a bunch of mumbo-jumbo but in fact vision is a concrete thing. There are techniques for developing a vision which you can learn and then put into practice. We know this in consulting from working on large complex organizational issues. We use vision as part of a serious management consulting practice to help executives get lined up and ready to execute what they have to do to succeed.

If you can't picture a different future, it will be hard to get there. Mental pictures are powerful for drawing us towards something new but the picture has to be positive. Imagine that you are sitting in an all-white room, white carpets, white silk furniture. Out of the corner of your eye, you see a little child toddling over with a big wobbly glass of bright purple grape juice. If you picture the spill, I bet it will happen. If you picture a smooth path into your firm hands, I bet it will happen. We can will our career in the same way.

I was tooling away for a huge electric utility in the eighties as a management consultant. During a first-time vacation to California, I sat in San Francisco airport and said to my partner, 'I am coming back here. I want to do business here.' A few weeks later, I got more serious about visioning and here is the trick to achieving a positive vision. First, you need a quiet space. Second, you need to say in the present tense, 'Here is what I am doing, this is who I am doing it with, it feels like this.' In other words, visioning isn't sitting there saying I would like a change or I want to be somewhere else. On the contrary, to make vision work, you have to say emphatically and with great conviction, 'I am in this place, it feels and looks like this. I am surrounded by these kind of people.' So the vision I began to craft for myself went something like this:

'I am working in a company that is dynamic and full of energy. There are young people. It is lively. There is a tangible product. I go to California on business.'

A few weeks went by and I got a call from a headhunter. Unbelievably, he told me about a job with none other than the famous jean-maker, Levi Strauss and Company. Young, dynamic, fantastic product and headquarters in San Francisco. I knew the job was mine because I had dreamed it. Spending time on the vision is a prerequisite to dreams coming true because when opportunities present themselves, you know they are right for you. Things just click into place and make the leap possible. In fact, there is a lot of comfort associated with the move since you have spent so much time in the present tense living it. Vision warms us up for better things. You may be thinking this is once in a lifetime but it isn't. I have made vision work for me throughout my whole career. I think vision is powerful. Try it and tell me how it works!

Concentrate on your vision for at least six months. See what happens. Keep reminding yourself of the picture. Like a puzzle, some pieces will fit and others won't. Keep refining the image.

Set goals

There was a study looking at the power of career goals that took place at Yale University in 1950. This found that of that year's graduates, only 3 per cent had taken the time to write down their goals. A follow-up study of the same class taken 25 years later, in 1975, found that the 3 per cent with written goals had accumulated more than 90 per cent of the entire group's wealth (AGRA Address, Graduating Class of Ryerson Polytechnical Institute, 1999).

Sometimes I like to poke fun at multimillionaire Anthony Robbins, the ultimate American icon for success. He has a television show and a series of home video/audio tapes that are guaranteed to make you successful. He seems a parody of himself. Tall, tanned and handsome he dishes out his homely mantra of 'goals plus action every day'. Actually, it is true that if you set goals and take action against them, you will get further ahead than the majority of people who just sit back and keep thinking about things. So he's not wrong.

The big difference, and I say *big* difference, is that you have to work on developing your skills and talent so that you can succeed. It's not all action planning.

snap, crackle or stop

Visioning exercise

Here is what I am doing …	Describe the kind of work you are doing – look hard but don't worry if it isn't precise. What does it feel like? What are you thinking about?
I am in a place that feels like and looks like …	Try and picture the environment – what is it like? What is the atmosphere? How do you feel there? What are the conversations about?
I am working with people who are …	What kind of people are you in contact with? What kind of people do you love working with? Are you working alone?
I am living here …	Where are you located? What does it look like, feel like?

Work on this picture. When you have worked on it, actually take a piece of paper or an index card and write out your vision. Make the picture as complete as you possibly can. Stare at it, work with it over a period of a few weeks. What is working, what isn't?

Once you have enough of a picture in your mind, the next step to getting there is commitment, plain and simple. Very few people will admit to being lazy. The kind of commitment I mean is 100 per cent undiluted determination. People often ask me for help in their career, I make the time *provided* they commit to the hard work.

Go and get a reality check on your dream jobs

The consulting profession has taught me the power of interviewing. It is through interviews with our key clients that we are able to help organizations and people make the kind of change they require to succeed. Theory is good but people are better. People are the ones who can provide us with a wealth of knowledge and information. So in this search for a different kind of work and career, it is essential to get out there and talk to people. You can use your feet or your hands. You choose. Don't let geography stop you. Wherever you are, you can certainly use your digits to call people up. Find people on the internet, in newspaper articles and on television. Contact them and ask them for time.

It is a gift for most people to give advice.

Some people get hung up on making these kind of calls. They feel beads of sweat at the thought of contacting strangers or people they don't know so well and asking for help and information. You are going to have to get over this. The first few calls might be difficult but trust me it gets easier with practice. What you have to understand is that people generally love to talk about their passion and work. It might be people you admire, people who do what you want to do. You might be surprised at how easy it is to conduct these interviews, and they often provide other contacts you can later enlist for support in making the actual change.

Plan your own field trips. Go and find out what other people are doing. Check out the environment. There is nothing like being right there, up close and personal to see what it's really like.

If you need a script, then consider planning in advance before making the call. As you pick up the phone and hear that little big voice of yours saying with a whine, 'But I don't want to do this,' talk back to yourself and say, 'Who asked you anyway?' Here are a few tips for making a successful, informative interview call (you can also send an e-mail):

◆ Introduce yourself.

◆ State the objective of your call – to get some information and advice.

- Ask for what you want – I would like 20–30 minutes of your time.
- Set a time right there and then.
- Conduct the call and celebrate.

When working on the business book *Shared Services: Mining for Corporate Gold*, I contacted very famous writers, heroes of mine in the business world, for an interview. Surprisingly, many said yes, Rosabeth Moss Kanter and Peter Block to name but two. Even Warren Bennis returned my e-mails but unfortunately declined. So it pays to try. Nothing to lose really and I learned a lot.

Is it talent, hard work or both?

Talent is part born and part worked on. Even if you are born with it, are you able to recognize it? Tiger Woods is the greatest golfer in the world. He has combined the strength of the long game with the finesse and delicate elegance of the short game. Above all he is known for having the mental strength it takes to be a winner. There's no question the man has a wealth of inner talent but he has also persevered and dedicated his life to improving his skills. He did not just step up to the tee and become a world-class champion overnight. Every day, he gets up and goes out to practise. Tenacity makes all the difference.

Talent scouts say they can spot winners by the amount of focus and hard work the candidates display early on. People who succeed do the work. The point is you will not be perfect in your chosen field, you will not get it right the first time. It's a question of tenacity and sticking with the work. Even if you don't emerge as a genius in your field, you can still be very good. You can still be better than you are today.

Anyone interested in having their work published will have the idea of rejection drilled into their brain by all of the wonderful self-help books there are available on how to get published. When rejection slips came to my address, I actually felt good because I knew that at least I was further along the path of being able to master destiny than the rest of the people who were still just toying with the idea but hadn't taken any concrete steps towards the achievement.

At the very heart, you have got to be good at what you dream of doing. Now that doesn't mean you have to start out perfectly.

Anyone who has ever written a computer program, a piece of music, a book, or someone who has sculpted, built a house, invented something will tell you that practice makes perfect. At the core of it all is the need to work your talent to the degree that you can find out whether you are any good or not.

Working at the craft is what will help you succeed.

The only way to find out if you have talent is to do and then see what people think. You can't be discouraged if your first foray doesn't yield the appropriate results. The old saying, 'if you don't try, you'll never know' works to define the conundrum. People who are successful in finding the right career don't walk around smugly thinking they are smart and talented. They may admit to having talent but all will talk about the hard work. Yoshiko Shinohara is president of TempStaff Group, the second largest temporary agency in Tokyo. She staked $4,000 of her personal savings in 1973 to start the company and taught English by night to pay the bills.

There is no such thing as an overnight success. It is easier for cynics to focus on the idea that talent is born not developed, as this provides an easy excuse for choosing not to do anything, not to try and see if you have what it takes. Perhaps the toughest part is committing to the hard work involved in defining what it is we want to do with our lives. We are always looking for that one great business idea out there, the one that will just fall into our laps and be a hit. Most of the time, our destiny is right under our noses. Get up and go to your personal bookshelf, what kind of books are there? How do you spend your time when given a chance? What's your background and experience? How can you use it? How do you know what your talents really are? The competence with which you carry out your current job gives you a strong sense of security. The dreams are a little more frightening.

Design your own apprenticeship

Part of the process includes the need to improve your talent. You have to think about creating your very own apprenticeship scheme that has one goal in mind: learning the trade or art of your desires. This means working at improving the talent or working at creating the business you've been dreaming of. Unless you stop what you are doing or find a way to improve your talent while working, you'll be exactly where you are today in one year from now.

You don't have to have perfect talent to make it. There are loads of people who are smarter, who did better in school, who are even brilliant who have not managed to find their destiny-type career and are wasting away at a job that is underwhelming. Pure talent is not the answer, it is perseverance at the end of the day. Obviously it's easier if one is brilliant and has lots of fat juicy talent but it isn't necessarily the key ingredient to success. Like Amy Tan says, 'Inspiration is often just hard work.' Getting to where you want takes time and an investment in your own development. The new corporate mantra is 'individuals are responsible for their own career'. Well the same goes for finding your passion. Take charge and work on improving your talent pool.

Apprenticeship schemes are the cornerstone of all the trades we know today. You don't suddenly pick up a bunch of wrenches and hang out a sign saying plumber. It takes knowledge, practice and time working under a master to develop the skills and talent. For those involved in the creative arts, working at the craft is a lifelong affair. There is no one right time when you step out into the limelight as if to say 'I am ready now, I am sufficiently talented to be seen in public.' Working at the craft may mean several job hops. You can't always get from A to B in a straight line. As a matter of fact, you almost never get there in a straight line. All you have to do is give yourself one hour of every day to work on your future. The hour must be spent developing your talent. After one week, you'll have increased your talent and skill by investing seven hours. After one year, you will have invested 45.5 days in developing your skill. That has got to make a difference.

- Who is a master in the career of your choice?
- Where is the absolute best place to study in your subject area?
- What companies are known for attracting the best in this talent area?
- How many years and what kind of experience will you need?
- What skills and knowledge are you missing, how are you going to develop them?
- What books do you need to read to improve your talent?
- Who can you shadow?

Shadowing is an ideal way to get close to the action. It is like auditing courses at university where you are allowed to sit in but not write the exam or get a credit. Same concept here. Ask someone, a master in your chosen field, if you can spend some time shadowing them on the job. You may find that it is not all that it is cracked up to be. A nurse friend of mind was restless to change careers when an opportunity came up to work as an extra in a feature film being made at her hospital. After one weekend of waiting around for her big ten-second moment where all you can glimpse is her eyebrows over the surgical mask, she gave up her dream and kept on nursing. She did eventually give it up and is now a landscape architect. It took going back to school and considerable sacrifice. But she's happy.

Taking action is just committing to one step

When people begin to dream about other possibilities, about opening up a business, going back to school, owning a store etc., the fear lurking at the back of the mind is the secret question of whether they have what it takes or not. Although visioning is a great tool for increasing motivation and helping to move you forward, it is essentially not enough. You need action. But it doesn't have to be one gigantic mother of an action plan. No, it just has to be one step. Do one thing towards your future every week. How hard is this? It means making one phone call, going to meet one person, one internet search, one association, one new article, one book.

Do one thing towards your future every week.

The biggest motivation for taking a step should be the consideration of what it will be like to live with yourself and being disappointed for not giving it a try. How will you feel next year, or in five years, if you didn't have the courage to make the right move? What kind of regrets will you have and how deep will they be?

Can you afford not to change anything? The answer is no. Find a way to make money and have a life too. There's no such thing as ever having enough. Get used to this. If you are a habitual worrier, try curbing your spending. Recognize that money tricks us into deception. We can start to justify our crummy existence at work when money is our only goal. In fact, when we only work for money, we often spend too much: buying things becomes a consolation for our lousy existence. So we have to watch out that career choices are not made for financial reasons alone.

If you don't use your body, you'll never make the change. You have to actually get up and do something. You can't get anywhere from a seated position. Get out of your head and begin to make connections and phone calls. Go places. Talk to people. Make the change with your feet. Action is what makes it happen. You know all this but you have to start now. If you wait any longer, you're reducing the chances of success. Time is passing by.

10

chapter ten
snap, crackle or stop:
the finale

take charge and make it happen

I do believe we have the power to master our own destiny. It comes down to choice and accepting our responsibility for getting what we want. Forget about luck. Take charge and make it happen. Make that change you've been thinking about. Get into your state of mind, figure out where you are and what you can do about it. My government friend who quit her job to go into her own events planning business leaned over to me on an airplane a few weeks ago and asked, 'Why didn't you tell me how great this would be?' Well, what can you really say? How can you tell someone how thrilling it is to be in charge of your own career? Even if the business doesn't work out and she goes back to a corporate job, she will have mastered her own destiny for ever.

Have you snapped yet?

If you've already snapped, you know the current job is over. It is time to make that change you've been thinking about. I know you are scared, we all are. I know you don't know what the next career is, just that today is no longer an option. First of all, you've got to give yourself credit for accepting the truth. You are now in the place called no return: this is great, it's half the battle. You have entered the zone of possibilities. However, don't take the first thing that comes along. Think long and hard about what it is you really want to do deep down. Give in to your dreams, and let your imagination take you to exciting possibilities and don't censor yourself. Understand that you have snapped for a good reason. Don't settle back into complacency, justifying why today is pretty good after all. Keep telling yourself you have made the right decision. To summarize:

◆ The status quo really is over.

◆ Accept that you are 100 per cent right about this.

◆ Be determined to focus on the next phase of your life.

◆ Do not justify the good news about your current career.

◆ Set a deadline and stick to it.

You are really on your way. When you're at work, imagine yourself outside of the action, looking through glass at everyone going about their busy work. Know that you are on the outside. Be detached; stay focused enough to do a good job but don't be so obsessive. If you are used to working long hours, cut back, find time to think. Tell yourself over and over that you are right, that your instincts are unfailingly correct. Don't start finding all the good things about your current situation. Your future is not necessarily more of the same thing. Accept the good stuff as good but begin seeing it as something that belongs in the past. When you start thinking about the people and friends you have made, understand that your real friends will still be friends when you move on.

Your number one job is to focus on the future.

Think about how to get from here to there. You may be thinking of resigning, or you may be thinking of getting another job while you are working. Hold on to all those possibilities. Act on them and I guarantee the opportunity will present itself. If you want something badly enough and you spend time thinking about the future, sooner or later you'll be given the chance to make it happen. If you are a beginner at this, you are going to be astonished. For some reason, it always works easiest the first few times you try it.

Finally, set yourself a deadline for action, plan when you want to be in a new situation. You can always make revisions but deadlines will help to give you resolve. They will force you to carry through on your thoughts and make sure that you do act. The final date will propel you into action, and will cause you to take more steps than you might normally as you watch the weeks go by, getting closer and closer to the big one.

Crackle – that quiet discontent

If you are in this state of mind, you know that some days are good and some are not so good. You may not even be unhappy, just restless, wondering if there isn't something else out there. Looking at others, you may think everyone is in the same boat, that this state of mind is normal – and it is normal. The question is what to do with the rumbling feelings that surface from time to time. Do you act on them or sit tight? If you want to get ahead, you'll probably have to move.

You could adopt the following approach that alters depending on what kind of day you are having. On the more disquieting days, hold the thought that you are right and there is something else you are supposed to be doing with your life. Give in to your belief that you have not found the right outlet for your talent and expression, and begin to consider other possibilities. Seek out the ones with ideas who seem to be genuinely more satisfied with you. Find out if it's true or just an act.

On the days where your job feels just right, give in to that idea and figure out how you can get even more satisfaction from where you are today. Don't think of throwing everything out of kilter. You don't have to make a move. It may be right under your nose right now and you are missing it. Your current work situation may offer the ultimate possibilities for self-expression, so consider how you can get more of what you want from your current job. Consider the following:

- Accept that something is missing.

- Figure out how to plug the void.

- Ask yourself if you can fulfil this search for expression during weekends and in your spare time.

- Accept the right to be more satisfied than you are today.

- Actively court change even if you decide to stay put.

Remember the old consulting saying, 'If you are feeling it, it's there.' Imagine then that something is missing from your life. Try and get a handle on what is missing. What do you want more of from work? Less of? What are the times in your working life when you are exhilarated? Figure out how to increase the time spent in this area. Ask yourself if the void can be plugged some other way. Could volunteer work give you what you're looking for, can hobbies and interests consume you in a way that leaves no aching void? I look at people with a passion for things like old cars, food, collecting clocks, working with needy people and it is clear that these activities are all consuming – they provide such a passion that work is secondary.

Try and accept the fact that work can have that same outlet for expression and be a place where passion is lived out every day. Imagine that you have a responsibility to yourself to try and find as many outlets for expression as you can in a lifetime. If golf is your passion, can you imagine creating a role for yourself in the golf world?

When there are little feelings of discontent, it is essential to actively court career change on a regular basis. Keep up your network; don't stop looking at the classified ads for jobs; keep on learning and talking to people who can help you in your next career move. You will make many changes in your lifetime so if you want to be in control of your own destiny, you will have to constantly take charge. Don't ever rest on your laurels. Today's job may not even exist in the future. So always be ready for change.

Stop – get out of the zone

If you are here, you are marking time, stuck in a rut and not connected to your next career. This is a vulnerable place: you run the risk of being fired or left out to pasture. The best thing you can do is get yourself ready. Imagine you are being fired. Now what will you do? If you can afford to quit your job, it would give you a chance to think about what next.

Getting off the treadmill is guaranteed to create change provided you are realistic about your own skills. Get outside people to tell you honestly whether you are the kind of person who will be able to come to a wholesale stop and then find something else. Listen hard to people you trust and take their advice. I cannot prescribe stopping as the one and only way for change but it definitely works. If you are going to quit, take out some insurance by leaving the door open to come back, not necessarily in your old job but in some kind of capacity. If you have a good reputation and leave before you have lost your energy, you'll be in a good position to go back should you want to.

If you have been stopped by other events, or someone else in your life, you need to take the time to get comfortable with what has happened. You are not alone. Many many people have been pushed before their time so take advantage of the advice and expertise about dealing with traumatic change that is out there. From a destiny standpoint, you may find that it turns out to be the best thing that ever happened to you.

Consider the following:

◆ Do not jump at the first thing that comes along, no matter what.

◆ Give yourself time to remember what you wanted out of life.

◆ Seek allies in your quest.

◆ Work hard at possibilities.

◆ Shadow opportunities.

Intellectually you will know the danger of jumping from the frying pan into the fire. Imagine your old self as just that, a shadow. Leave it behind while you pursue new ideas. Develop a circle of coaches and mentors who will support you should emotions and fear take over. If you have already let go of one job and are suspended in that in-between place, you will be getting worried and may find yourself grabbing at the first straw that comes along. See if you can leave the country and camp out somewhere where it will be impossible to do this. If you can't leave, then build your own retreat – try and avoid situations and people that will ply you with possibilities exactly like the job you just left. Cut yourself off for a while, culitivate new friends and contacts.

Your challenge is to find enough time to remember what it was you always wanted to do with your life. Look to your interests and your past for clues about the kinds of work you want to be doing. Seek allies who share your view that taking the time to find work in your destiny line is worth doing. Surround yourself with new thinkers, the ones who will challenge conventional thoughts about careers. Work hard at investigating possibilities. If you are able, try and find opportunities to shadow people working in those careers you are thinking of. Find out how you can discover more out about these kind of careers.

Get as close as you possibly can to new kinds of work and opportunities. Even if you decide eventually to go back to the same line of work that you were previously in, you'll be better off for it.

The dream versus the reality

Things will not work out quite like you imagine, but that's okay. The point is not getting to one specific place, it is evolving towards a series of possible destinations. Downhill ski instructors claim to help people overcome their fear by gradually increasing their tolerance to heights, moving scared skiers up the mountain a bit at a time. For someone who thinks people are crazy for strapping two planks to their feet and hurling themselves down a cliff, I for one can relate to the idea of gradually moving up towards the sky. Nothing ever is exactly like we imagine. It's just the idea of getting closer. People mastering their own destiny don't see themselves at the end of the line.

But you do have to permit yourself to dream and to accept the fact that you owe it to yourself and the people around you to find work that uses your talents. It is legitimate to seek happiness and since we spend so much of our waking lives at work, it is all the more important to get it right.

Accept that now is the right time

You are almost never too old to search for destiny even though there are a few limitations. Medical schools typically don't accept students over 40 years old. But this is not the norm. Most of us can begin right now to find the work that is the ultimate expression of our talents. But we have to accept that now is the right time. As Nelson Mandela says, 'Our deepest fear is that we are powerful beyond measure. It is our light not our darkness that most frightens us.'

Make the war for talent work for you. If you are lucky enough to be one of those people working in the knowledge sector, you have what everyone is looking for. So start acting like it. You can take a year off and get close to the action you're seeking. You can try something else and come back to the old job market if you have to. If you want to try self-employment, then what have you got to lose? If you just want a change to a really different job within your own company or industry, then what are you waiting for?

Smart companies are going to get this idea if they want to hang on to good people. You might have to help them in this by leading the way. Organizations want us to be mastering destiny with them. If you're not getting a chance to stretch your talents at work, then prod your bosses in the right direction. Owners of companies want their staff to be as exhilarated and as committed as they are. The question is, what are they prepared to do to give people really meaningful work? How are they going to create an environment that really is fun?

Repeat after me: *this is exactly the right time, tomorrow won't be any different than today.* Don't make excuses for inaction. Decide what you want and jump in.

It is up to you

I think we are on the brink of a real movement in the work world. I believe that more and more people are openly admitting their unhappiness. More and more people are taking control and walking out when there is no link between work and satisfaction. Oh sure, a lot of people are still blaming their companies judging from the results of most employee surveys. In reality, it is up to you and me to take control of our destiny and find the work that is the best expression of our talents. Yes, people can help us but in the end it will be you and me.

And yes, if companies were smart, they would work with this dissatisfaction and be more flexible in their approach. Helping people find destiny and the right outlets for their expression is going to be a winning formula for both parties. There are no formulas that will tell you exactly what you should be when you grow up. Mastering destiny by definition means accepting responsibility and recognizing that the answer lies within us. We can look outside for inspiration but in the end we must be the ones to seize the idea and make it happen.

Make your company a proposition – contract with them to either give you a leave of absence, let you study while working, work part-time while you pursue your passions, or whatever it will take to make you feel happy.

Remind yourself that you are one unique individual in this world. You have a lot to bring to the party even if you don't know where the party happens to be right now. Destiny is not one location, you will have many opportunities to find work that is fulfilling and an expression of your hopes and dreams. It is the reason you and I exist. Repeat after me: *I am going to find as many outlets for expression as I can possibly jam into my life. I am going to do it. I am going to make that change that gets me closer to my destiny. I just have to.* Come along with me, take the power and write your own destiny, and have the courage to get into the game. Promise me you won't be in the same place doing the same thing next year. I make the same promise to you. The momentum is out there, let's go for it.

appendix one
the inventory

Complete the inventory by choosing which phrase best describes you. Please select one response only only even if two responses seem to fit.

1 What's important to me in a career is a company that values:
1) loyalty
2) independence
3) development
4) expression

2 I believe I can get what I want:
1) somewhat sceptical
2) if I plan correctly
3) if I focus
4) if I am open

3 I believe I am basically in the right career:
1) not sure
2) yes, but could do better
3) questioning if this is so
4) absolutely

4 I am at the stage in my career where money:
1) seems to be hard to come by
2) is never really enough
3) is not as important as it was
4) seems to come naturally

5 I see my work as fulfilling:
1) not as much as I want
2) to a degree but I'm capable of more
3) for the most part
4) completely

6 I identify with what I do for a living:
1) not really
2) most definitely
3) not as much as I used to
4) completely

7 When I have to tell other people what I do for a living I feel:
1) neutral
2) proud
3) tentative
4) excited

8 When it comes to the next step in my career:
1) I don't know what it should be
2) I am thinking about what it should be
3) I am open to what it should be
4) I don't worry about what it should be

9 I spend time every day thinking about my future
1) not really
2) sometimes
3) a lot
4) all the time

10 I would describe myself in relation to my career as:
1) happy
2) relatively happy
3) neither happy nor unhappy
4) extremely happy

11 I am restless in my career:
1) somewhat
2) most of the time
3) constantly
4) very little

12 I believe I stand a better chance of getting what I want if:
1) I care enough
2) I take charge
3) I focus
4) I am open

13 People at work would see my role as one that:
1) seems just beneath my skills
2) plays to my strengths
3) is in transition
4) seems to be perfect for me

14 I trust intuition over logic to make career decisions:
1) not as much as I should
2) sometimes
3) usually
4) always

15 I am:
1) more qualified than the job requires
2) very qualified but could be more so
3) figuring out what qualifications I need
4) perfectly qualified for what I am doing

16 I am known for taking risks with my career:
1) rarely
2) sometimes
3) a fair amount
4) a lot

17 When things I do at work go wrong I try to:
1) understand it
2) analyze it
3) learn from it
4) accept it

18 One of the primary drivers for work is:
1) necessity
2) career growth
3) personal growth
4) expression

19 My friends think my career is:
1) not where it should be
2) on the right path
3) great and wonder why I'm questioning things
4) what makes me who I am

20 I like my current job because:
1) I feel relatively happy
2) it is an important step in my career
3) it is providing me with lots of options
4) I am certain of being in the right field

21 Many days at work, I feel like time:
1) could be better spent
2) is well spent
3) is running out
4) flies

22 I am exploiting my talents:
1) I wish I was
2) I am to a degree
3) I am somewhat
4) I am doing as much as I can

23 My job enables me to express my interests:
1) some of the time
2) most of the time
3) not as much as it should
4) almost always

24 My skills and experience match up to my ambition:
1) about right
2) somewhat
3) a fair amount
4) completely

25 I would prefer to be:
1) working in a better job
2) getting more recognition
3) doing something different
4) doing more of the same

26 I see my career as:
1) stalled
2) not going fast enough
3) unclear
4) just right

27 My job is a place where I am:
1) not using enough of my skills
2) using my skills
3) questioning my skills
4) focusing on my skills

28 In my spare time I tend to:
1) forget about work
2) have fun
3) explore new things
4) invent new things

29 People would say I like to:
1) stay in my comfort zone
2) stretch my comfort zone
3) explore my comfort zone
4) get out of my comfort zone

30 I can continue doing the same kind of work provided that I continue to:
1) be competent
2) contribute
3) evolve
4) create

31 The person I am at work is:
1) a bit different from the person I am at home
2) very different from the person I am at home
3) somewhat the same as the person I am at home
4) the same as the person I am at home

32 I spend time thinking about my career in terms of whether it fits with:
1) my life
2) my goals
3) my development
4) my needs

33 When it comes to career change:
1) I wait for the right timing
2) I try to control the timing
3) I consider when is the right time
4) I know when it is the right time

34 I feel most energized:
1) when I am at home
2) when I am at work
3) when I can balance work and home
4) at work

35 If a new career opportunity presented itself, it would be important that the job was something:
1) that would be a good use of my skills
2) that would provide for advancement
3) that developed my skills
4) that focused my skills

36 My energy is :
1) drained
2) being used properly
3) scattered
4) focused

37 In my work life I have:
1) done similar work
2) had a few different jobs
3) had around three or four different jobs
4) had many jobs

38 I find routines:
1) comforting
2) necessary
3) help me focus
4) too predictable

39 I feel like I am working on my passion:
1) very little
2) somewhat
3) 50/50
4) most of the time

40 I am at the point in my life where:
1) I have achieved what I can
2) I need to achieve more
3) I need to do something else
4) I am doing what I want

Score your inventory

To score your inventory add up the number of times you chose 1, 2, 3 or 4, and write those numbers in the box below.

Quadrant 3 Number of times you selected # 3. _____	Quadrant 4 Number of times you selected # 4. _____
Quadrant 2 Number of times you selected # 2. _____	Quadrant 1 Number of times you selected # 1. _____

Mastering invention (3) **'Working for learning'** I am experimenting with my talent My job is making me restless I want to take more risks I am trying to overcome fear I am overwhelmed by options I am trying to change I am not sure who I want to be	**Mastering destiny (4)** **'Working for passion'** I exploit my talents My job is making me happy I take risks I feel empowered I am doing the right thing I am not fearful about change I am doing what I want to be
Mastering convention (2) **'Working my way up'** I use my talents My job is getting me somewhere I plan my risks I am independent I value my potential I don't think I need to change I know what I want to be	**Mastering institution (1)** **'Working for a living'** I don't use my talents enough My job is something of a necessity I am afraid to take risks I am dependent I undervalue my potential I am afraid to change I don't know what I can be

Mastering institution

When mastering institution, we are in a stage of our career where the job is basically a practical necessity. Work in and money out the other side. We don't expect the job to fulfil us in any deep and meaningful way. It is a time of trying to please others more than ourselves, a time for doing what is right. The job offers us an opportunity to make friends and develop relationships. We basically want to keep our heads down, not rock the boat too much. We assess the job for how it fits into our life – does it have the right hours, is it in the right location? This state often makes us feel relatively tied down with few options. It feels more like survival than anything. It is a time when we don't have a strong identity with our career.

Mastering convention

When mastering convention, we are in a stage of our career where the motivation is primarily to move up the career and social ladder. The focus is independence;

planning carefully how best to spend our energy, who and what to spend it on. In this career state, we tend to cultivate relationships for what they can do for us. We think of career change in analytical terms, deciding what the next move will be. During this stage, we may take jobs that stretch our talent and intellect but we tend to avoid deep personal change. We think we are saving that for later. It is a time for amassing wealth and material things. It is a time when our 'at work' and 'at home' personalities are often quite separate. This is because we are developing a strong identity and brand in relation to who we are in our careers.

Mastering invention

When mastering invention, we are in that stage of our career where we are guided in our career choices by what we can learn rather than what money or title we get. We are starting to question our whole life and how work fits in (or doesn't). Our selections are governed by our self-identified needs for development, not whether it is moving up the career ladder. It is a time for cultivating diverse relationships and friends in order to broaden the learning. In this state, there is a tendency for us to scatter our energy. We generate too many options and possibilities; we have too much on our plate. We often find it difficult to get beyond the thinking stage and into action. We have many ideas but may not find the energy or time to actually do anything about them. It is a time when we are developing an identity around what we learn, not what we are doing.

Mastering destiny

Mastering destiny is a stage of our career where career choices are guided by our need for expression. We don't just think about possibilities, we act on them. It is a time of feeling empowered and courageous about taking the next step even when we don't know where it will lead. This stage in our career is one where we are completely self-motivated and require no one else to prod us into working. It is a time when we have come to trust our talents, when we know our strengths and weaknesses better than anyone. The identity at work and play is the same. There is knowledge that we would be spending our last day at work doing what we are doing for a living. It is a time of constant energy directed towards our passion.

There's a delicious myth about the writer Margaret Atwood. The story goes like this. Margaret is standing in an elevator with a neurosurgeon after doing the keynote speech at a medical convention. The neurosurgeon looks over at Margaret and says, 'You know I'm going to write a book myself when I retire.' To which Margaret clipped back, 'Yes, I'm going to try my hand at neurosurgery once I'm finished writing books.' If you're not in it for passion, you're not in it. How insulting of the good doctor to imagine her craft as a post-career afterthought.

appendix two
self-assessment tools

Myers-Briggs Type Indicator® (MBTI)   The MBTI inventory is a widely used personality inventory. It helps you to make important life and career decisions by allowing you to better understand your unique personal qualities.

The MBTI has about 93 items and takes about 30–40 minutes to complete. Using the results you can determine preferences on four scales:

1 Extroversion–Introversion
2 Sensing–Intuition
3 Thinking–Feeling
4 Judging–Perceiving

The various combinations are then used to suggest career options you may wish to pursue given your personality type.

Business Career Interest Inventory (BCII)   Developed at the Harvard Business School, this inventory clarifies your unique pattern of interests and then uses this information to define a range of possible careers in which you could find a way to express those interests. It is premised on the concept that interests, not skills, should be the foundation for people's careers.

Campbell Interest and Skill Survey (CISS)   The CISS measures self-reported vocational interests and skills. In addition to identifying interests, it also reports your confidence level in performing occupational activities. This instrument focuses on careers that require post-secondary education. It has about 320 items and takes 35 minutes to complete.

Strong Interest Inventory® (SII)   The SII measures your interests in a broad range of occupations, work activities and leisure activities. It is based on the idea that you will be more satisfied and productive when your work is interesting. The results of the inventory give you career choices based on your interests and from these you can explore different career options. The SII has 317 items and takes 25 minutes to complete.

Learning Style Inventory – Hay/McBer Training Group, Experience Based Learning Systems   Originally developed by David Kolb, this inventory describes how to deal with career choices based on your orientation to learning. There are four types of learning: diverging, assimilating, converging and accommodating. Interesting cluster of careers to choose from.

Career Occupational Preference System® (COPSystem)   The COPSystem measures an individual's abilities, interests and values and relates the scores to 14 occupational groupings. The COPSystem takes about 30 minutes to complete and the results suggest occupational preferences which you can investigate.